# DJing for Beginners

# DJing for Beginners

## Mixing, Beatmatching, and Scratching with Vinyl, CDs, and Digital Tracks

MATT ANNISS

*amber*
BOOKS

Published by
Amber Books Ltd
74–77 White Lion Street
London
N1 9PF
United Kingdom
www.amberbooks.co.uk
Appstore: itunes.com/apps/amberbooksltd
Facebook: www.facebook.com/amberbooks
Twitter: @amberbooks

ISBN: 978-1-78274-373-6

Project Editor: Sarah Uttridge
Designer: Brian Rust
Picture Research: Terry Forshaw

Printed in China

# CONTENTS

# INTRODUCTION

This book is designed to help you get started as a DJ. We'll help you to select appropriate equipment, learn tricky techniques and offer advice on how to use these skills to entertain crowds of people. By following our advice, you'll be well on your way to mastering the art of DJing.

## PIONEERS OF THE GROOVE

Ever since the release of the Technics SL-1200 vinyl turntable in 1972, DJing has been driven by technological advancements. That deck was revolutionary, because it featured a pitch control fader, so that DJs could speed up or slow down the records they were playing. Pioneering DJs soon worked out that they could use two Technics turntables, alongside a specially made DJ mixer, to create seamless musical blends where the beats never stopped. This became known as beat matching, and remains the foundation of DJing to this day. Early hip-hop DJs also used the same Technics turntables to create new tricks and techniques that they called 'scratches'. In this book, we'll take you through the basics of both beat matching and scratching.

### Frankie Knuckles
*Some DJs play a vital role in developing new styles of dance music. 'The Godfather of House', Frankie Knuckles, did this in the mid-1980s. The 'house' sound he championed is now the main form of dance music.*

### Technics SL-1200
*The iconic Technics turntable was initially designed and put on sale as a home record player. Instead, it was adopted by DJs, who liked its sturdy build and pitch control fader – a unique feature at the time.*

Anyone who has ever devoted time to DJing will happily tell you how addictive it is. There is something particularly rewarding about blending songs together to create a unique musical performance. Most musicians have to make do with a limited number of notes, chords and melodies, but DJs have a potential library of millions of tracks to choose from. These can be combined in an almost limitless number of ways, meaning that no two DJ sets need ever be the same. Because of this, DJing offers music lovers true artistic freedom.

This has been emphasized in recent years by advancements in DJ technology. Now, there are a huge number of different options for would-be DJs, from the tried-and-tested methods of old – namely, using turntables and vinyl records – to cutting-edge computer software solutions that include extra functions to spice up your sets.

**Sasha at the Hacienda, 1989**
*During the 1990s, British DJ Sasha became one of the first superstar DJs, as in demand in Australia and the United States as in the UK and Belgium.*

**Steve Aoki**
*Steve Aoki is one of a new breed of superstar DJs who play digital music files using their laptop and a digital vinyl system. This has helped make Aoki one of the world's richest DJs. According to Forbes magazine, he earned $24 million in 2014 alone.*

## EVEN MORE OPTIONS

Today, fewer DJs use vinyl turntables. Instead, some DJs choose to use CD turntables, many of which are also capable of playing MP3 files stored on portable USB drives. Others prefer using laptop computers loaded up with DJ software, sometimes with the aid of a special piece of equipment known as a DJ controller. In this book, we'll explain how to perform key DJing techniques using all of these methods.

There's more to DJing than simply technical skills, though, so we'll cover other important topics such as how to build and organize a music collection; how to DJ in front of a crowd of people; and how to build and develop your DJing career. We'll even outline further steps you can take to personalize your DJ sets, such as creating unique versions of songs or producing your own from scratch.

**Pioneer CDJ-1000**
*Launched in the early 2000s, the Pioneer CDJ-1000 was as revolutionary as the Technics 1200. By emulating the feel and control of vinyl DJing, it made DJing with CDs appealing to a wide range of DJs.*

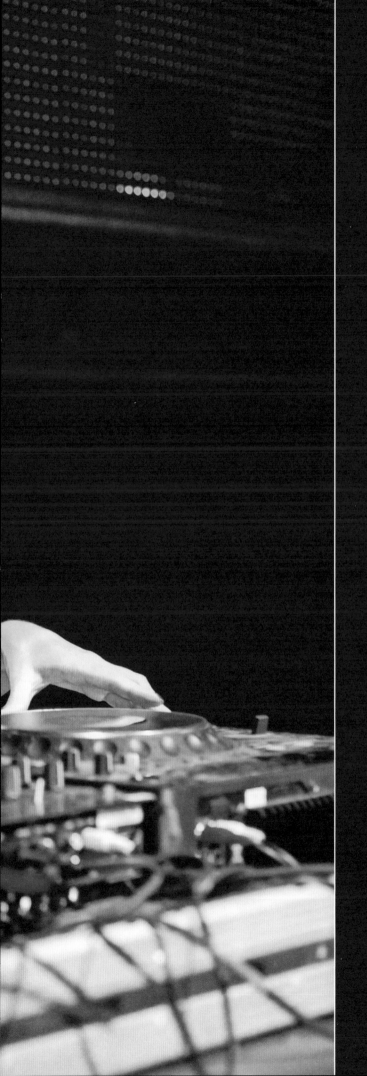

# CHAPTER 1:

# DJ BASICS

Before getting into the nuts and bolts of DJing technique, you'll need to get set up with some equipment to practise on. To help you decide what to buy, this chapter focuses on the pros and cons of different methods of DJing, outlining the gear to get... and what to avoid.

**LEFT:** Today, many DJs choose to use next-generation CD turntables, which are often also capable of playing music files stored on portable USB devices.

# WHAT YOU NEED

Some of these items, such as a DJ mixer, headphones, and an amp and speakers, are essential. Whether you need vinyl turntables, CD turntables or a laptop with a digital vinyl system/ DJ controller will depend on the DJing method you choose. We'll explain these options over the next few pages.

## VINYL TURNTABLES
**(PP. 14–15)**

## MUSIC
**(PP. 86–105)**

## DJ MIXER
**(PP. 30–31)**

## CD/USB TURNTABLES
**(PP. 16–17)**

# DIGITAL DJ CONTROLLER
## (PP. 28–29)

# LAPTOP & DIGITAL VINYL SYSTEM
## (PP. 18–19)

# DJ HEADPHONES
## (PP. 32–33)

# HI-FI AMPLIFIER & SPEAKERS
## (PP. 32–33)

# CHOOSING YOUR METHOD

Before you can learn to DJ, you need to pick your method. While some DJs use a combination of equipment – for example, playing off both vinyl and CD turntables – it's easiest to pick one set-up and focus on that. Here are the four most popular DJ set-ups.

### DJING WITH VINYL RECORDS

This is the method most commonly associated with DJing, and the one on which most of today's tried-and-tested DJ techniques were developed. It has been around since the 1970s, and requires connecting two DJ-friendly vinyl turntables (specifically those with speed, or 'pitch', controls) to a DJ mixer. Many established DJs prefer the sound and feel of vinyl DJing, but building up a collection of vinyl records can be an expensive pastime.

### DJING WITH CDS AND PORTABLE USB DRIVES

CD turntables, commonly referred to as 'CDJs' thanks to Pioneer's industry-standard range of professional players, have been around since the 1990s. Today's CD turntables are far more technically advanced, with functions that help emulate the feel of vinyl turntables, and tools to help DJs unleash their creativity. Some CD turntables are also able to play MP3 files. Like vinyl turntables, CD turntables must be connected to a DJ mixer.

**Vinyl (above)**
*Many thought vinyl DJing would die out following the MP3 revolution, but it remains popular with DJs of all ages.*

**CDJs (below)**
*This set-up would be expensive if you bought it all new, but you can get used equipment for a fraction of the price.*

## DJING WITH DIGITAL VINYL CONTROL SYSTEMS

Digital vinyl systems (DVS) combine traditional DJ hardware with 21st-century computer technology. At the heart of the DVS is a software package that runs on a laptop computer. With the aid of a special audio interface, DJs can control MP3 files stored on their laptop, using regular vinyl or CD turntables. Although DVS software includes many additional creative tools, tracks are mixed using traditional equipment and techniques.

**Digital Vinyl Systems (left and below)**
*DVS hardware is great for those who want to combine the feel of traditional vinyl DJing with the potential of digital DJing. However, it can be expensive for beginners, as you need to buy a lot of equipment.*

**DJ Controller (below)**
*There are many models of DJ controllers so, before you invest in one, spend some time online comparing features and prices.*

## DJING WITH A DJ CONTROLLER

A DJ controller is a special piece of hardware designed for use with DJing software, such as Virtual DJ, Serato DJ or Traktor Pro. It contains buttons, knobs and faders to control many different aspects of the software. Tracks stored on the computer are mixed using the controller, which often looks like a redesigned version of a traditional DJ mixer. For beginners on a budget who already own a laptop, DJ controllers can be a great option.

# DJING WITH VINYL

Once upon a time, all DJs plied their trade with a stack of vinyl records, two turntables and a mixer. While plenty still prefer this method, choosing vinyl isn't necessarily the best choice for beginners in the 21st century.

If you choose to DJ with vinyl, you're really choosing to join the culture of record collecting and 'crate digging' – a popular term to describe hunting for vinyl – that surrounds it. If you commit to learning to DJ with an all-vinyl set-up, you're also committing to devoting time and money to building up a record collection.

## WAX MANIA

That's not to say that acquiring records has to be an expensive pastime. So many records were manufactured and sold during the format's heyday that you can find plenty of older albums and singles quite cheaply on the second-hand market. Search online, and you'll also find plenty of sellers offering bundles of records, often in dancefloor-friendly styles of music, to help bulk out beginners' collections. If you opt for a vinyl set-up and don't already own records, this is worth considering; you'll need records to practise mixing with, after all.

**Second-hand Wax**
*Because vinyl records have been a popular music format for more than half a century, you can find previously owned copies of older releases in all sorts of places. Charity shops, record fairs and second-hand stores are great places to find vinyl at rock-bottom prices.*

**Mix and Match**
*A vinyl DJ's set-up is not complete without a mixer and a good-quality pair of DJ-friendly headphones. When looking for a mixer, don't get dazzled by flashing lights and extra features – good sound and build quality are more important.*

**Changing Times**

*At one time, you would find Technics turntables in every venue that employs DJs. Although vinyl DJing remains popular, some clubs have ditched vinyl decks in favour of CD turntables.*

## TURNTABLES

The beating heart of any vinyl DJ's set-up is a pair of turntables. Ask a DJ to name their favourite turntable, and 99 times out of 100 they will mention the Technics SL-1210 or the older SL-1200. More than 3.5 million of these famously reliable decks were built between 1972 and 2010, and they remain in use at many clubs. In January 2016, a special edition 50th anniversary version of the SL-1200 went into production, with a price tag of several thousand pounds. Happily, you can easily find second-hand original models for £400–600 ($600–900) per pair. Other models of DJ-friendly turntables are available, at a variety of prices. Whether you buy brand new or second-hand turntables, look for direct drive models. These are a little more expensive than the belt drive ones often marketed at beginners, but they are far easier to mix with and much less likely to break. If you want to learn to scratch, you'll need a direct drive deck.

**Stanton T.62**

*If you can't stretch to a second-hand pair of Technics, manufacturers such as Stanton offer decent alternatives that can be bought new for the same price, or less.*

# DJING WITH CDS

These days, far more DJs use CD turntables than vinyl decks. This is due to their ease of use, the reliability of modern CD decks, the ability to also play MP3 files, and the fact that the equipment is now found in almost all clubs.

### INDUSTRY STANDARD

Since the launch of the Pioneer CDJ-1000 in 2001, tabletop DJ CD players have dominated the market. These feature a large jog wheel, designed to mimic the feel of DJing on vinyl turntables. Today, even budget CD turntables include a jog wheel as part of their control system, although how they feel and operate differs. You can learn to mix CDs with any tabletop player, although you are still likely to encounter Pioneer models if you play in clubs.

**Numark NDX200**
*Budget CD turntables, such as this Numark model, don't feature as many functions as expensive Pioneer CDJs, but the basic controls are very similar.*

**Pioneer CDJ-900 Nexus**
*This is the CDJ-2000's little brother. It features fewer functions and costs significantly less, but still boasts almost everything you'll need to create exciting, interesting mixes.*

All of these are good reasons to choose CD turntables, but there are downsides, too. The CD decks found in venues are usually high-end professional models, such as Pioneer's industry-standard CDJ-2000. Brand new, these cost nearly £1,500 ($2,300) each, putting them beyond the reach of most beginners. There are, thankfully, plenty of cheaper options available from a wide variety of manufacturers, though functions, build quality and control systems vary significantly.

## GOING DIGITAL

Other features to look out for when selecting CD decks include the ability to play digital audio files (MP3, WAV) off a data CD, and a USB port to plug in a portable hard drive. In some ways, today's CDJs are as much digital music players as CD turntables.

## PREVIOUSLY OWNED MODELS

When making a decision on which CD turntables to buy, it's worth considering second-hand models. If buying a pair of brand new CDJ-2000s or CDJ-900s is beyond your budget, you might be able to find a pair of older CDJ-1000s or CDJ-800s for a much more reasonable price. These might not include MP3 or USB capability, but they will allow you to mix CDs while getting used to the control system and key functions.

**USB Stick**
*It is possible to buy portable USB sticks with very high storage capacity. You can store hundreds or even thousands of MP3 music files on one tiny, pocket-sized device.*

**Pioneer CDJ-2000**
*This is becoming an increasingly common sight in clubs. The fact that two players can be connected by an Ethernet cable to play MP3 files off a single USB stick is one of its most popular features.*

**Burn Your Own CDs**
*Many DJs choose to burn their own CD-Rs of songs they've bought and downloaded from the Internet. It's these discs that fill up their bulging CD wallets and provide musical ammunition at gigs.*

**DJ TIP:** Learning to mix on CD turntables is hugely worthwhile. Many DJ controllers and MP3 turntables are modelled on CD turntables, with similar features and control functions. Once you have mastered CD mixing, you will be able to use a wide range of equipment.

# DJING WITH COMPUTER SOFTWARE

If you are on a budget and own a laptop computer, opting for DJ software could be the way forwards. You can mix using your free or inexpensive MP3 files, and the software offers more creative options than standard DJ equipment. Crucially, there are also lots of different programs to choose from.

Many DJ software packages offer the option to mix tracks using the laptop's trackpad and keyboard, but most DJs prefer a more hands-on system. For this reason, many manufacturers have developed dedicated DJ controller hardware. These vary in design and price, but contain everything you will need to mix songs together, and get the best out of the software. Not as many club DJs opt for a laptop-and-controller set-up – not least

**Stand Up**
*Many DVS DJs (see p19) invest in a foldable laptop stand. It is a wise purchase, as it will allow you to set up your laptop in any DJ booth, regardless of size. You'd be surprised how small many club DJ booths are!*

**Ready To Go (above)**
*Most DJ controllers come bundled with DJ software, vastly reducing the amount of money you need to spend. As long as you already have a laptop computer, controllers are a great all-in-one option for beginners.*

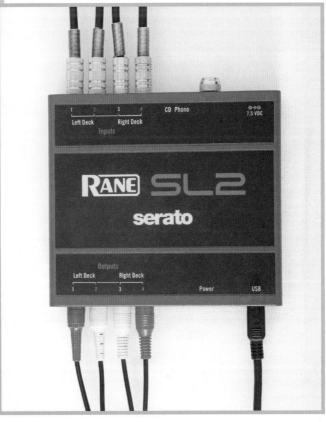

# PC OR MAC?

DJing software is available for both Apple Macs and Windows PCs, so you can probably use your existing laptop, if you have one. If you're buying a laptop, look for one with USB ports, a large hard drive (for storing music), and good processing power. More processing memory means the DJ software will run more smoothly.

because it's a lot of equipment to carry around – but it is certainly becoming increasingly popular.

## DIGITAL VINYL SYSTEMS

Another popular method of DJing with computer software is to use a digital vinyl system, such as Serato DJ or Traktor Pro. These systems act as an interface between your computer and existing DJ technology, namely vinyl or CD turntables (bottom left). They allow DJs to mix songs stored on their computer, using equipment commonly found in clubs. A DVS offers the best of both worlds, although the cost is often prohibitive for beginners who don't already own any DJ equipment. We'll explain more about using DVS, DJ software and controllers later in the book.

**Rane SL2**
*It's easy to pick up Rane Serato DVS equipment second-hand, for cheaper prices. If you're going to do this, opt for SL2, SL3 or SL4 models; the older SL1 boxes don't work with Serato DJ, the manufacturer's latest software.*

# PAUL OAKENFOLD

## 1963–

**RECOMMENDED LISTENING:**
*Resident: Two Years of Oakenfold at Cream* (DJ mix, 1999)
*Perfecto Presents: The Club* (DJ mix, 2005)

Paul Oakenfold was arguably the world's first superstar DJ. Long before the likes of Skrillex, Calvin Harris and David Guetta became household names, Oakenfold was jetting around the globe, performing DJ sets in front of thousands of people. Nearly 30 years on from his breakthrough, he remains one of the biggest DJs on the planet.

Oakenfold made his name in the 1980s, first as a DJ pushing early house music, and later as a dance music producer. Alongside studio partner Steve Osborne, he produced the Happy Mondays' pioneering dance-rock album, *Pills, Thrills & Bellyaches*. It was a huge success, earning them a chance to deliver dance remixes of tracks by U2, Simply Red, New Order and many more.

It was through his skill as a DJ that Oakenfold really made his mark. At a time when dance music was becoming hugely popular, he was famous for playing at the best venues, and to the biggest crowds. In the late 1990s and early 2000s, Oakenfold was the headline attraction at countless dance festivals, and at emerging 'superclubs' such as Ministry of Sound in London and Cream in Liverpool. By now, he had turned his attention to trance music, pushing a style that would later turn Tiesto, Paul van Dyk and Armin van Buuren into international stars.

More significantly, Oakenfold was the first DJ to tour the United States in the style of a pop star or rock band. From 2000 to 2001, he criss-crossed the United States, performing DJ sets in front of crowds of thousands. He's been in demand around the world ever since.

**Clubland Pioneer**
*Oakenfold's rise as a DJ began during the late 1980s when he was also promoting club events in London. His Spectrum and Land of Oz parties at the Heaven nightclub were among the first to champion acid house music in the UK.*

FAVOURED STYLES:

**TRANCE**
**PROGRESSIVE HOUSE**
**EDM**

# CHAPTER 2:
# EQUIPMENT EXPLAINED

By now, you should have chosen your DJ method and invested in an equipment set-up. Next, we'll take a closer look at the features and functions of some key pieces of DJ hardware, helping you to become more familiar with the controls.

**LEFT:** For beginners, DJ equipment can seem complicated and confusing. While many mixers, controllers and turntables boast a large number of functions, the basic controls are actually very easy to pick up.

# TURNTABLES

Before you can throw yourself into DJing, you need to understand the equipment you will be using. We'll start by taking a close look at the main features of a DJ-friendly vinyl turntable.

**1** On/off switch

**2** Stop/start button

**3** 7-inch single adaptor holder
Some 7-inch singles were manufactured with a large hole in the middle, to fit jukeboxes. If you buy a 7-inch adaptor and keep it here, you'll be able to play those kinds of singles.

**4** Revolutions per minute (RPM) buttons
During the manufacturing process, vinyl records are pressed at one of two speeds (33 or 45), measured in revolutions per minute (RPM). This is, quite literally, the number of times the turntable platter rotates in a minute. Check a record's label to find the RPM.

**5** Platter
This is where the record sits. During playback, the platter spins continuously. Lightly touching the side of the platter with one or two fingers will momentarily slow it down a little. DJs often use this trick to perform slight adjustments during the mixing process.

**6** Spindle
This central spindle is attached to the platter, and helps keeps the record in place. It can be tweaked with two fingers to momentarily speed up playback. Again, this is a trick some DJs use while mixing.

**7** Target light
This pop-up light can help you see where you're putting the stylus on the record, prior to playback. It is particularly useful in dark environments, such as clubs.

### 8 Pitch control fader

This is the most important feature of any DJ turntable. It allows you to speed up or slow down the platter in order to get the record in time with one playing on another turntable. To slow the platter down, move the fader upwards (away from your body); speed the platter up by moving the fader downwards (towards your body). The numbers on the side signify the percentage change in platter speed.

### 9 Headshell, cartridge and stylus

The stylus is a diamond needle that reads the grooves pressed onto the vinyl record. It is attached to a cartridge, which is in turn screwed into the headshell. This fixes onto the turntable's tone arm via a locking mechanism. To avoid damaging your records, you should change the stylus every six months or so.

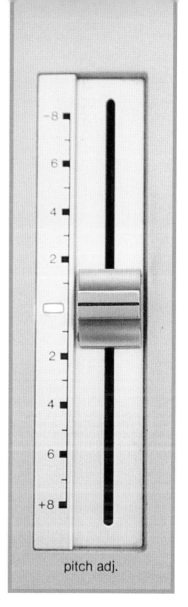

pitch adj.

**Technics** QUARTZ
Direct Drive Turntable System SL-1200MK2

pitch adj.

### Needles

Turntables read the grooves on vinyl records using a diamond-tipped needle. Over time, these needles wear down and can damage your records if you don't change them.

### Up and Down

Be careful when changing the speed of records. Increasing or decreasing the pitch of a record to plus or minus eight can dramatically change the way the song sounds.

# CD TURNTABLES

CD turntables are a little more complicated than vinyl ones, with more features. Here, we've concentrated on the key functions of Pioneer's range of CDJs. Check the instruction manual of your particular turntable for in-depth explanations of its functions.

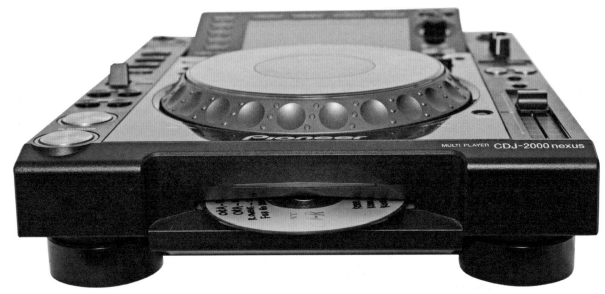

**Front Loading**
*Almost all CD turntables are front loading, with a CD slot on the front panel of the unit. That is usually the opposite end to the display panel.*

**In the Slot**
*On some Pioneer CDJ models, it is possible to insert a USB drive into the player, and then play the songs contained on it on a second turntable. To enable this function, two CDJs must be connected using an Ethernet cable.*

**1 USB SLOT**
This function is not available on all CD turntables, but is a key feature of modern Pioneer CDJ models. When a USB drive is plugged in, MP3 files can be played and manipulated in the same way as tracks contained on a CD.

**2 DISPLAY**
This includes, among other things, the current speed, in beats per minute, of the track being played, and, depending on what time mode is selected, how long there is left of the song.

**3 JOG WHEEL**
On a CD turntable with vinyl emulation (such as the Pioneer CDJ range), the jog wheel can be used to scratch, hold and release a track (as you would when cueing a record on a traditional turntable) and perform other tricks. As on a vinyl turntable, you can nudge or gently pull back the outer portion of the jog wheel to perform minor speed adjustments.

**4 JOG MODE CONTROLS**
These buttons allow you to switch between two control methods: vinyl emulation and CDJ, which is closest to what you will find on other CD turntables.

**5 TEMPO FADER**
Like the pitch control fader on a vinyl turntable, this can be used to increase or decrease the speed of the track being played. Some CD turntables also allow you to alter the range of this speed adjustment, in order to radically change how slow or fast a song is.

**6 TRACK SELECTION BUTTONS**
The top two buttons allow you to flick through the CD in order to find the right track. Use the bottom two to quickly scan through the song itself, in order to find the right starting point (for example, a kick drum sound).

**7 PLAY/PAUSE BUTTON**

**8 CUE BUTTON**
Press this while a track is paused, or held in position using the jog wheel, to set a new start point (known as a cue point).

**9 CD SLOT**

# DIGITAL VINYL SYSTEMS

Despite the name, digital vinyl systems (DVS) are compatible with both vinyl and CD turntables, and in some cases standalone DJ controllers. DVS packages contain some very specific equipment not found elsewhere in DJ set-ups.

### AUDIO INTERFACE

This is the beating heart of any DVS system. It acts as an interface between turntables, a laptop running DJ software (usually Serato DJ or Traktor Pro), and your DJ mixer. Audio leads from vinyl or CD turntables are connected to the inputs, with a USB lead running to the laptop. Audio leads run from the interface's outputs to the inputs on the back of your DJ mixer (see below).

### TIMECODE CONTROL DISCS

DJs who opt to use DVS systems do not need to take a large volume of records or CDs to a club. Instead, they turn up with a pair of 'timecode' discs (either vinyl, or CD), which are then used to play music stored on their computer. It certainly makes traveling to gigs much easier! You can find a detailed explanation of how DVS systems and timecode discs work on page 73.

**Timecode Care**
*If you played the same record over and over again, it would soon begin to wear out. The same is true with DVS timecode control records (above). For this reason, DVS DJs are advised to change their control discs every six to eight months.*

## DJ CONTROLLER

Popular DVS packages such as Serato DJ and Traktor Pro also support DJ controllers, which can be used to mix as an alternative to vinyl or CD turntables. It is usually possible to use a MIDI controller, more often associated with music production or live performance, as an alternative. We'll discuss this in greater detail later in the book.

**Mission Control**
*The Serato branding on this Hercules DJ controller signals that it was designed for use with that software package. Many controllers are built with a particular software package in mind, but are actually compatible with all major DJing programs.*

**Sound Cards (above)**
*The audio interfaces sold as part of the Traktor Pro DJ package, such as the one above, can also be used as an external sound card for your computer. This is particularly useful for those keen to try their hand at music production.*

# DJ MIXERS

The humble mixer may not be particularly glamorous, but it is arguably the most important piece of kit in any DJ's set-up. It is with the mixer, after all, that you blend the sounds that audiences will hear.

### 1 CHANNEL FADERS

Each sound source – vinyl or CD turntables, basically – is plugged into one of two channels, each of which has its own volume control fader. Push the channel fader up to increase the volume of its specific sound source.

### 2 CROSSFADER

The crossfader allows DJs to switch between the two channels. If the crossfader is set to the left and the channel one fader is pushed up, you will hear what's being played on that source. If both channel faders are pushed up and the crossfader is set to the central position (midway between left and right), then you'll hear both sound sources.

### 3 EQ CONTROLS

These give you more control over the specific sound coming out of each channel. The 'low', 'mid' and 'high' names correspond to the sound frequencies that can be tinkered with. Turning down the 'low' EQ, for example, will vastly reduce the level of a song's bassline and drumbeats.

### 4 PRE-FADE LISTEN BUTTONS

Sometimes called 'cue', 'preview' or 'PFL' (short for 'pre-fade listen'), there's one per channel. Move the fader or press the relevant button to hear the sound coming into that channel from its respective turntable, using a pair of headphones. The PFL controls are a key feature of DJ mixers, allowing you to listen to a song before or during a mix.

### 5 HEADPHONE MONITORING CONTROLS

Most mixers have two of these. One is simply to hear the volume in the headphones. The second allows you to either hear a mix of the 'master' sound the audience hears, and something you're cueing up (using the PFL fader or buttons), or – as is the case with this mixer – quickly switch between 'master' and 'cue' options. Together, these can also be used while mixing to monitor what the audience hears.

### 6 MASTER AND BOOTH CONTROLS

The 'master' volume is what the audience hears. The 'booth' volume is only used when a separate speaker for the personal use of the DJ is connected (for example, in a club's DJ booth).

### 7 BACK PANEL

This is where you connect your turntables. There are inputs for each channel, with separate choices for vinyl turntables ('phono') and CD decks/ DJ controllers ('line'). The 'master' output is used to connect the mixer to your amplifier and speakers.

**Connections**
*The back panel of the mixer is used for plugging in the musical sources, such as vinyl or CD turntables. Each channel includes two sets of inputs: one for vinyl decks ('phono'), and one for other digital equipment (CD turntables, a DJ controller, or the outputs from a DVS box).*

## Mixer diagram

MIC

PGM 1

PGM 2

LEVEL    OL    HIGH         GAIN         GAIN         HIGH         MASTER

HIGH                                                              AUX OUT

EQ                                        EQ

LOW                                                              PHONES LEVEL

FlexFX      FlexFX

MID          LOW          LOW          MID          LOW

AUX IN

L   PAN   R          DRY    WET          L   PAN   R          MASTER / CUE

TTM 56
PERFORMANCE MIXER

innoFADER          CHANNEL REVERSE          PGM 1   CUE   PGM 2

REVERSE          TRANSFORM          RANE          TRANSFORM          REVERSE

MODE 1          innoFADER          MODE 1
MODE 2                              MODE 2

FAST                                                              FAST

CONTOUR          MONO PGM1 / PGM2          CONTOUR
                 STEREO HOUSE

SLOW                                                              SLOW

+10
+7
+4
+2
0
-2
-4
-7
-10
-20

REVERSE   MODE 1   MODE 2

A                    B

### Differences

*The Rane mixer we've used in this book is just one of a vast number of models available to buy. While most boast similar functions, the way they are laid out and used may vary slightly. Check your mixer's instruction manual if you are unsure about any of the functions.*

# INs & OUTs

The vast majority of DJ equipment, including both CD and vinyl turntables, connects to a mixer using RCA phono cables. These all feature distinctive red and white connectors at each end of the lead, which in turn plug into the colour coded sockets on the back of your equipment. Most mixers can also be connected to a home amplifier and speakers using an RCA phono cable. Professional level mixers may also feature XLR or 'quarter-inch jack' inputs, in order to connect them to club sound systems.

**XLR plug and socket**

**RCA plugs**

**1/8th Jack plug**

# EXTRAS & ADD-ONS

Once you have your basic DJ set-up sorted, take a more serious look at accessories. Some, such as a good pair of DJ headphones, are essential, whereas others are optional, or can be picked up at a later date.

### DJ HEADPHONES

It is impossible to mix without them, so headphones should be one of the first pieces of kit you buy. DJ headphones come in a number of designs, though it's the 'close back' (sometimes called 'close cup') ones that you should opt for. These completely cover the ears, making it easier to hear them clearly in noisy club environments. As they'll be on your head for hours, try to find a pair that are comfortable to wear for long periods. If the sound they produce is loud and clear, even better. Prices vary, but expect to have to pay upwards of £100 ($150) for a good-quality pair.

**Sennheiser HD-25s**
*These are arguably the most popular DJ headphones on the market, renowned for their durability and good-quality sound.*

### SLIPMATS

If you've decided on a vinyl set-up, you will need a pair of slipmats. These are round felt mats that allow you to hold a record in place while the turntable platter spins below. New turntables often come bundled with slipmats. If not, they can be picked up fairly cheaply from any DJ store.

**Different Designs**
*Slipmats come in all sorts of different designs, often featuring the name and logo of well-loved record labels or other lifestyle brands. Some companies also offer a customization service, printing your design directly onto the cloth used to manufacture them.*

## MONITOR SPEAKERS

The one crucial element of any DJ's home set-up that we've not previously mentioned is a set of monitor speakers. For most bedroom DJs, an amplifier and home hi-fi speakers will suffice. If you're feeling flush or want louder sound, it is possible to buy powered monitors. These are standalone speakers, designed for club use, that feature a built-in amplifier.

### Boxes Versus Bags
*You can buy a sturdy record box capable of storing 50–100 records, but if you prefer something that is easier to lift or carry around, then go for a bag. Manufacturers such as Magma and UDG offer well-made bags capable of holding up to and including 100 records.*

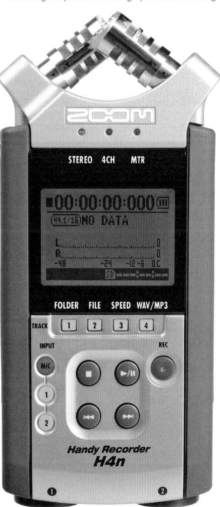

### Mix Analysis
*Recording your home mix sessions, using a portable digital recorder then listening back to them, can be a good way to learn. You'll soon start to recognize what you did right and wrong, and which songs go together well.*

## RECORD BAGS, BOXES AND GIG BAGS

As you would expect, these come in all sorts of shapes and sizes. Vinyl DJs who play out a lot will need a rugged record box or well-made bag – those by UDG and Magma being popular choices – while digital DJs (those who use laptops, and DVS or controllers) are catered for with specially designed gig bags.

## CD WALLET

If you've chosen to mix with CDs, then a high-capacity CD wallet is essential. The good news is that DJ-friendly CD wallets capable of storing between 100 and 300 discs can be picked up relatively cheaply from online stores.

### Mixed Formats
*Some DJs enjoy playing with a mix of vinyl and CDs. If you're one of those, you could make do with a small CD wallet that fits neatly into your record box or bag.*

## PORTABLE DIGITAL RECORDER

Once you become a little more experienced, a portable digital recorder is a good investment. You can use it to record demo mixes at home or to capture your club sets for posterity.

# NINA KRAVIZ

## Undisclosed–

**RECOMMENDED LISTENING:**

*Nina Kraviz* (album, 2012)

*DJ Kicks* (DJ mix, 2015)

Since breaking through at the tail end of the 2000s, Siberian Nina Kraviz has become one of the most widely respected DJs on the planet. She has achieved this feat by developing her own unique style of DJing, which blends old and new material from a wide range of underground dance music styles.

Kraviz first fell in love with house and techno music after hearing it on the radio in the 1990s, taking a keener interest when she moved to Moscow to study. While there, she wrote for a popular Russian dance music fanzine, learnt to DJ, and began to make music with a group of friends.

It was after attending the Red Bull Music Academy – an annual event for up-and-coming DJs, producers and electronic musicians – in 2006 that she began to realize that she could make a career out of her passion. She returned to Moscow and started putting on her own club events in 2008, slowly developing her DJ style while bringing big-name DJs from around the world to the Russian capital.

The same year, her first solo music productions came out, spreading her rising reputation a long way.

After releasing her debut album in 2012, she became a headline attraction at many of the world's most famous clubs, including Berghain in Berlin, London's Fabric, and Space in Ibiza. In 2015, she cemented her reputation as one of the world's best DJs with the release of the *DJ Kicks* mix CD.

**Label Owner**

*Like many DJ/producers, Nina Kraviz owns and operates her own record label, Trip. Launched in 2014, this releases dancefloor-friendly material from such artists as Population One, Steve Stoll and Kraviz herself.*

FAVOURED STYLES:

**TECHNO
TECH-HOUSE
DEEP HOUSE
ACID HOUSE**

# CHAPTER 3:

# MIXING BASICS

The next step on your journey to becoming a DJ is a big one. Like it or not, every DJ is judged on their mixing, which is the process of selecting and blending songs to create a seamless, non-stop musical soundtrack.

**LEFT:** A working club DJ runs her fingers down the side of the platter of one of the turntables she's using to mix. This is a trick used by vinyl DJs to subtly slow down a song to keep it in time with another.

# WHAT IS MIXING?

Once upon a time, DJs merely played songs one after each other, like a human jukebox. Then came Francis Grasso, a New York disco DJ with a revolutionary idea: why not mix the songs together to create one seamless musical performance?

It was an idea that would later take off, but only after Grasso had spent countless hours perfecting it during his sets at The Sanctuary nightclub. While the audience heard music being played on one turntable, he used headphones to cue up a song being played on another. When the time was right, he used a simple fader knob to blend the two songs together. Over time, he became skillful enough to blend the intros and outros of songs so that the drumbeat driving the dancers never stopped.

## DON'T STOP THE MUSIC

By today's standards, Grasso's mixes were rudimentary, but his 'seamless mixing' concept remains in use. Over the years, others have taken his basic techniques and elevated them to new levels. Some have even adapted them to create thrilling new ways of mixing records together. Throughout, the DJ's dedication to never letting the music stop has remained intact.

### Automatic
*Today, it is possible to mix songs together using the trackpad and keyboard of a laptop computer. Many DJ software packages also include sync functions, which when selected will mix two songs together for you.*

## MIX AND MATCH

The fact that there are many different ways to mix is what makes it so addictive. You can quickly flick between tracks to create an energetic performance (a method favoured by many hip-hop and drum & bass DJs), or layer tracks on top of each other in long, drawn-out blends. Alternatively, you can smoothly bring in a new song while another fades out, or overlay a beat-less passage of music over another record's rhythm track. Some DJs even combine all of these techniques, and more, depending on the situation or the sort of music they're playing. Once you have perfected the basic techniques, the possibilities are almost endless.

**Avicii**
*Like many modern DJs, Swedish EDM star Avicii prefers to use Pioneer CDJs, making the most of their equipment's USB ports, digital links and specially designed Rekordbox software.*

**Blurring Boundaries**
*Coki, who rose to fame as one half of dubstep pioneers Digital Mystikz, is renowned for a unique mixing style that blends traditional beat-matching techniques with the sort of scratch-happy turntablist techniques most often seen at the DMC World Championships (the world's leading DJ competition at which he has competed on a number of occasions).*

# PREVIEWING

Before attempting to mix, it is important to get comfortable with listening to tracks through your mixer. You can preview tracks in isolation, monitor the sound going out of the mixer, and even listen to both at the same time.

## THE HEADPHONE MONITORING CONTROL

This is a dedicated control knob that allows you to choose what you hear in your headphones. It can be turned to 'cue', 'master', or a mixture of the two.

## PREVIEWING A CHANNEL IN ISOLATION

Turn the monitoring control to 'cue' when you want a private preview of one of the channels. This is effectively the pre-mix setting, and is used by DJs while they are preparing to mix. You can decide which channel to preview by pressing its PFL or cue button.

**Design Differences**
*No two mixers are the same, and the way the previewing controls are laid out will differ from model to model. For example, the mixer shown in these tutorial pages features a button to switch between 'cue' and 'master', rather than a knob that allows you to hear a mix of the two in your headphones.*

### Buttons, Faders and Switches

*The mixer we're using in these photos doesn't have cue or PFL buttons above each channel fader, but rather a crossfader to switch between the two channels. If you're unsure of the preview controls on your new mixer, check the instruction manual. If you bought a used model, you may be able to find the manual online.*

### LISTENING TO THE MIXER'S OUTPUT

Turn the monitoring control knob to 'master' to hear what's coming out of the mixer. This only works, of course, if one of the channel faders is pushed up. If both faders are down, there will be nothing going from the mixer to your speakers.

### PREVIEWING A MIX OF SOUNDS

Turning the monitoring control to the midway point between 'cue' and 'master' allows you to hear a mixture of sounds: the channel being previewed (assuming you have turned on the applicable PFL button), and whatever is coming out of the master. This is a key function: as you progress to mixing, you'll be using it all the time.

**DJ TIP:** As you progress, you'll come across many different mixers, each with their own specific previewing controls. You'll soon learn to identify the location and style of these, and adjust your monitoring and mixing style accordingly.

# CONFUSED?

Getting used to the different ways of previewing sounds, and monitoring mixes, can be one of the biggest challenges. It's almost impossible to deliver killer mixes without using your headphones and the mixer's previewing controls, so spend plenty of time playing with the controls until you've found a sound level and set-up that you're comfortable with.

# CUEING

Whether you DJ with vinyl or CD turntables, before you attempt a mix you need to master the art of cueing. Put simply, this is finding the point of the song you wish to start from, before performing a mix.

Cueing up on CD turntables is easy, as the machine will automatically cue up the start of the song you've selected. You can set a different cue point by pausing the track at the moment you wish to start from and then hitting the cue button. The next time you hit 'play', the song will then start from this cue point. If you try this and accidentally cue up the wrong beat or note, use the in-track search function to adjust the start point. Once you've done this, hit 'cue' to set a replacement cue point.

Cue button

**Remove vinyl carefully from the sleeve**

**Hold the vinyl at the sides**

## HOW TO HANDLE VINYL RECORDS

To be able to cue up properly on vinyl turntables, you need to get used to touching records as they sit on the turntable. Eventually, it will become second nature, but to begin with it can be a tricky skill to perfect.

Records are fairly fragile, and in general need to be handled with care. When taking them from sleeves and placing them on a turntable, you should try to avoid putting your fingers on the surface of the platter. Once they're on the deck, all this changes. To cue accurately – and, in most cases, that means finding the start of a pattern of beats – you need to use your hand to move the record backwards and forwards, hold it in place, and then release it at the right time. The latter technique is known as 'dropping' a track, and is part of a process called slip cueing.

## SLIP CUEING ON VINYL

**1.** Put a record on and, as the first song kicks in, stop the vinyl spinning with the fingertips of one hand (if the turntable is to your left, use your left hand, and vice versa). The idea is to stop the record in such a way that the turntable's platter continues spinning below.

**2.** Slowly move the record backwards until you've reached the point where the first beat or musical note of the song begins, and then hold the record in place. When you're ready to 'drop' the track, give the record a tiny push and lift your fingers.

**DJ TIP: It takes time to perfect slip cueing, especially as you need to be able to do it accurately with either hand. Many DJs find it easier to 'drop' the track in at the right time if they slowly push the record backwards and forwards in time to the beat before releasing it.**

# YOUR FIRST MIX

Now you've got the hang of previewing and cueing tracks, you're ready to attempt your first mix. To do this, you will need to use your mixer's channel faders and crossfader to transition between songs.

Begin by playing a track on the turntable to your left. On the mixer, the channel 1 fader should be pushed up, the crossfader set to the left position, and the channel 2 fader turned down.

**1.** Using your headphones, preview and cue up a song on the right turntable. If you're using vinyl turntables, hold the record on the right deck in place with the fingers of your right hand. With your left hand, push up the channel 2 fader.

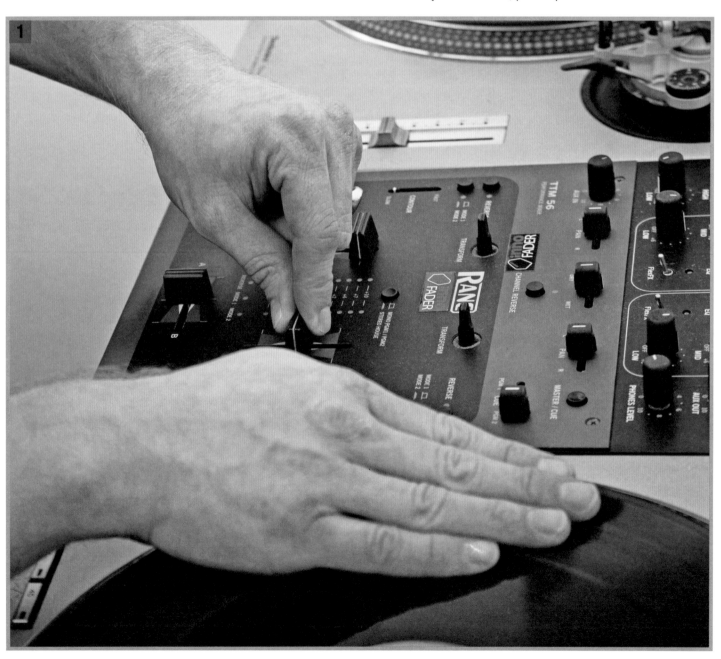

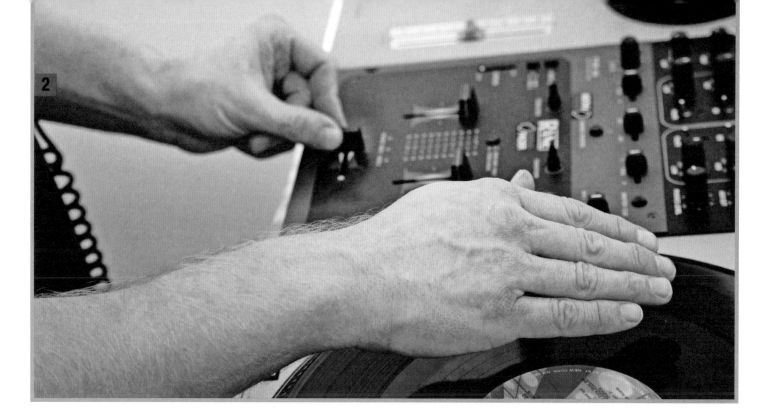

**2.** As the song playing on the left turntable begins to fade out, smoothly drag the crossfader to the right with your left hand. As the crossfader reaches the central position, drop in the track on the right turntable.

**3.** If you're using vinyl decks, release your fingers (remembering to give the record a little push as you do it). If you're on CD turntables, simply hit 'play'. To complete the mix, keep dragging the crossfader until it's fully set to the right. Congratulations: you've just completed your first mix!

**DJ TIP:** Spend some time practising these simple mixes until you're comfortable with the basic mixer controls and dropping in tracks from either turntable. To mix in a track from the left turntable, simply reverse the process described here. You could also try mixing with the channel faders alone. To do this, set the crossfader to the central position and practise pulling one channel fader down while you push the other upwards.

# SEAMLESS MIXING

Most people associate DJing with the ability to mix two songs together seamlessly, so that the drumbeats perfectly overlap. This technique is called beat matching, and it's arguably the most difficult aspect for new DJs to learn.

Beat matching involves getting the drum sounds of two tracks in time with each other, using your turntables' pitch control faders, before attempting to mix them. Songs rarely stay perfectly in time for long, so during the mix you may have to make some subtle adjustments to keep the beats synchronized.

Beat matching is a skill that can be perfected only through hours of practice. Even the world's best DJs still struggle with it from time to time, and it's not unusual to hear your heroes make little mistakes now and again.

**Use Your Ears**
*When you first listen to a blend of two different tracks in your headphones, it might sound like a complete mess. With time and practice, you'll soon start to identify the beats and other key musical elements of each track. Through this, you'll be able to work out what you need to do to get them in time, such as slowing one song down while speeding the other up.*

**BPM Counts**

*DJ software programs usually automatically work out the beats per minute of each song loaded into them. In this example, you'll find the BPM of each track listed, in blue, inside the circles at the top of the screen. Both tracks are 126 BPM, making them ripe for mixing together.*

## UNDERSTANDING BEATS

Most dance music tracks are produced with extended passages of 'open' drumbeats at the beginning and end, in order to make it easier for DJs to mix them together. To begin with, it is these intros and outros that you should concentrate on beat matching.

You can learn a lot by listening to these beats. For starters, you should be able to count to four in time with the drums. This is because most modern styles of dance music – house, techno, drum & bass, hip-hop, garage etc. – are underpinned by the same '4/4' beat. The pattern of drum sounds, known as the rhythm, will differ from song to song, but the underlying 4/4 beat will remain.

## BEATS PER MINUTE

By counting these beats, you can work out the speed, or 'tempo', of your songs. In dance music, tempo is measured in beats per minute (BPM). To work out the BPM of a track, simply count the number of beats you hear in 15 seconds, and then multiply this number by four. So, if you count 30 beats in 15 seconds, the song will have a BPM of 120.

Knowing the BPMs of your songs is key to beat matching. If you know that two songs are the same tempo, you will not have to adjust the speed much – if at all – to get them in time. If two tracks are several BPMs apart (125 as opposed to 120, say), you will have to adjust the speeds more to match them.

**DJ TIP:** There are a number of smartphone applications that will work out the BPM of songs for you. Tap the screen in time with the beats, and an accurate BPM will be displayed.

**BPM Display**

*When you load and cue up a song on a CD turntable, its BPM will be shown on the player's digital display.*

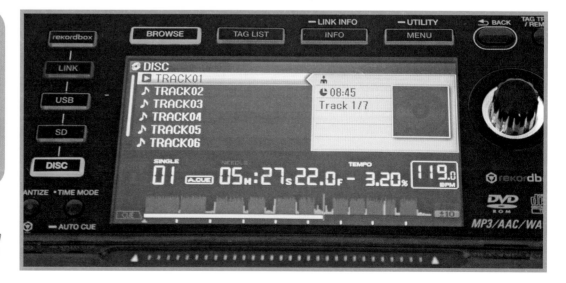

# BEAT MATCHING WITH TURNTABLES

It's time to put the theory into practice by attempting your first beat-matched mix. Before we begin, select two records with similar tempos, put on your headphones, and take your place in front of the mixer.

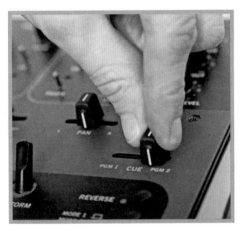

**Preview**
*The key to successful beat matching is careful monitoring, using the headphones and your mixer's previewing controls. This combination can be used before and during the mix to ensure that your mix is smooth and perfectly matched.*

Start by playing a record on the turntable to your left, ensuring that your mixer's channel 1 fader is pushed up so that music is coming out of the speakers.

Next, use the headphones to cue up the first beat of the record sat on the right turntable. Adjust the headphone monitoring control so that you can hear a mix of the track playing, and the one that you're about to mix in. Using slip cueing, drop in the second track. How does it sound? Is the second track faster or slower than the first? If it's slower, the beats will sound as if they are lagging behind those on the first record. Conversely, if it's faster, you'll hear the beats of the second record slightly ahead of those on the first.

**Speeding Up**
*Does the track you're about to mix in need to be a little quicker? If so, draw the turntable's pitch control towards your body. Try to keep the movement slow and smooth; if you do it too quickly, it will sound awful!*

**Slowing Down**
*If you need to slow down the song you're about to mix in to get it in time, then push the turntable's pitch fader away from your body. If the two songs are a similar tempo, you shouldn't need to slow it down too much.*

**On the Beat**

*You'll find beat matching becomes a lot easier if you manage to successfully 'catch the beat'. This means dropping in the second record so that the first beat – usually a heavy kick-drum sound – is perfectly in time with the other record. If you do this, you can then concentrate on keeping the two songs in time, and of course mixing them together.*

**Smooth Moves**

*When using the mixer's faders to blend two songs together, there are two approaches. The first is to move the faders slowly, to create a long, subtle mix. The second is to do the same movements quickly, for the mix to sound energetic.*

Try to get the beats as closely matched as possible by adjusting the speed of the second record, using the turntable's pitch control fader. To slow down the track, push the fader away from your body; draw it closer to you to speed it up. If the two songs boast a similar tempo, you won't have to adjust the speed very much. Be gentle on the pitch fader, as big moves in either direction can result in drastic changes in the song's tempo.

## GET READY TO MIX

When you are confident that you have matched the tempos of the two records, cue up the second record again, and hold it in place with your fingers. Now, concentrate on the first record, so that you can hear when the drumbeat outro begins. You want to 'drop' (and therefore let go of) the second record at the same time as this outro sequence begins. Give it a try: are the beats in time? If not, use the second turntable's pitch control to adjust the speed.

Once the beats of the two records are in time, it's just a matter of performing a mix, using your mixer's crossfader and channel faders. To begin with, concentrate on getting the transition between the records sounding smooth, while keeping both songs in time.

# BEAT MATCHING WITH CD TURNTABLES

Beat matching on CD turntables is arguably easier than it is with vinyl turntables. The process is fairly similar, although CD decks contain a few handy aids to make mixing just that little bit less stressful.

When you play a song on a CD turntable, its BPM will be shown on the player's digital display. This naturally makes matching the beats being played on two turntables a little bit easier. You will still have to use the headphones while previewing, cueing and mixing, but the BPM displays certainly speed up the process.

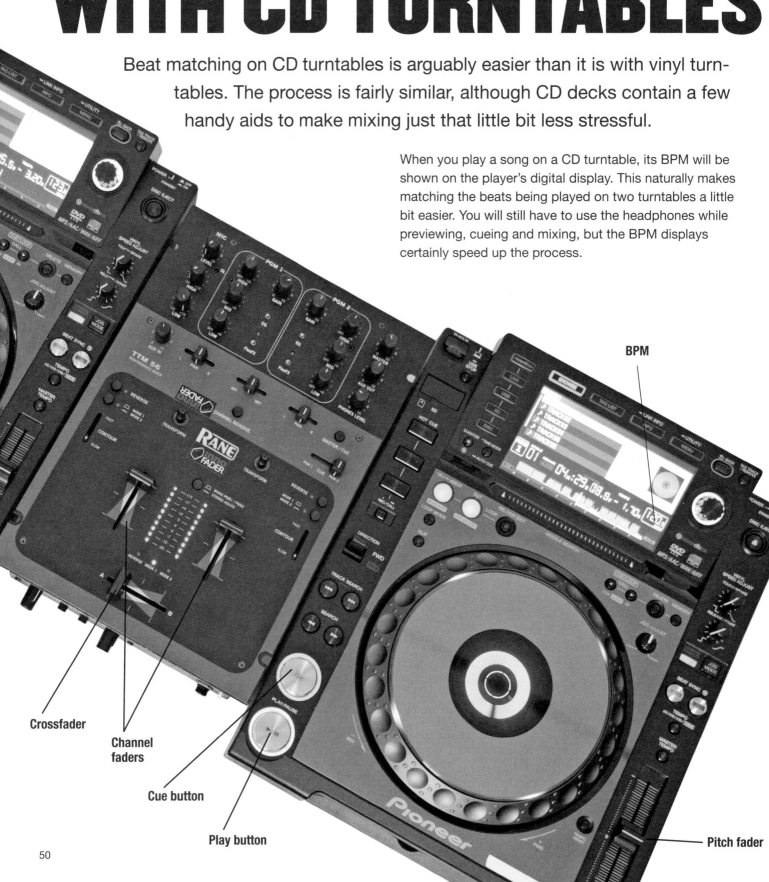

BPM

Crossfader

Channel faders

Cue button

Play button

Pitch fader

## PREPARING TO MIX

**1.** Set a track playing on the CD turntable to your right, and push up the mixer's channel 2 fader, so that sound comes out of the speakers. Next, turn your attention to the song on the left turntable. Use the in-track search function and the pause and cue buttons to set a start point.

Now focus on setting the BPM of the song on the left turntable, so that it matches the song on the right deck. Press play, and use the pitch control fader to adjust the tempo. As with vinyl turntables, moving the fader upwards slows the song down, while moving it downwards speeds it up. As you move

the fader, the BPM display will change. You'll be able to hear this change in your headphones, and check whether the two songs' beats match using the mixer's monitoring controls.

**2.** When you're happy that the BPMs are matched and that the songs are roughly in time, press the cue button on the left turntable to return the track to your chosen starting point.

**3.** As the song on the right turntable reaches its drumbeat outro, hit 'play' on the left deck. Use the headphones to check that the two tracks are in time. If they are, use the crossfader and channel faders to perform a mix. If not, use the pitch control fader to slightly adjust the speed of the song that you're mixing in.

# BEAT MATCHING WITH DVS

When using DVS (digital vinyl system) software, the way you beat match depends on whether you use vinyl or CD turntables. However, the information displayed on your laptop's screen makes getting songs in time much easier.

When you load up tracks in popular DVS software packages such as Traktor Pro or Serato DJ, you'll notice that the BPM of each song is displayed on each virtual deck at the top of the screen. You'll also see a visual representation of the song as a waveform. It's worth studying these waveforms in detail, because they give you useful info about the songs.

## UNDERSTANDING WAVEFORMS
Play a song, and the waveform will move in time with the turntable. Listen and look simultaneously, and you'll start to

> **DJ TIP:** Many DJs use split cueing. That means using one ear to preview a track on your headphones, while keeping the other free to listen to what's coming out of the speakers. You can try it by holding a headphone earpiece over one ear, while resting the other earpiece on your neck. Hearing different things in different ears can be confusing at first, but it's a skill worth mastering.

recognize where the beats appear in the waveform display. More often than not, the beat is represented by a taller wave. Different percussive sounds, such as kick drums (the heavier sounds that drive the track forwards) and snare drums (sharper, snappier sounds), look slightly different. Recognizing the difference will not only help you get two songs in time, but also match similar drum sounds.

**Check the Screen**
*You can gain a lot of information about the tracks you're mixing by looking at the software on your laptop's screen. Some DVS DJs use this to keep track of their progress while mixing.*

**Traktor Pro**
*Look carefully, and you will notice that the two tracks have vastly different tempos. The DJ will have to do a lot of work on the pitch controls to make the beats match!*

**Keeping Track**
*Digital DJs who use DVS become skilled at doing three things at once, namely using their hands to mix, their ears to listen, and their eyes to keep track of what's happening on their laptop screen. It sounds complex, but with practice it becomes second nature.*

## USING THE WAVEFORM DISPLAY WHILE MIXING

When you're playing two songs simultaneously on different turntables, waveforms will be displayed on each virtual deck on your laptop screen. Normally, you can choose how these virtual decks appear on screen – stacked up on top of each other, or side by side. Either way, you can see the waveforms next to each other, their BPMs, and whether the tall waves match. If they do, then it's almost certain that the two tracks are beat-matched, and therefore ready to be mixed. While mixing, feel free to glance at the screen – while monitoring on headphones, of course – to help keep track of the mix.

**Options**
*In Serato DJ, and other similar DVS programs, you can decide how you want the waveform display to appear. Some DJs prefer the waveforms side by side like this, whereas others prefer them stacked on top of each other.*

# DEADMAU5

## 1981–

**RECOMMENDED LISTENING:**

*4x4=12* (album, 2010)

*Album Title Goes Here* (album, 2012)

With his trademark giant mouse-head helmet, Deadmau5 is one of dance music's most recognizable figures. By using multimedia versions of this distinctive headgear during performances, the DJ has turned his sets into impressively flashy and immaculately choreographed stage shows.

It was some time during the early 2000s that Canadian DJ/producer Joel Zimmerman chose the Deadmau5 (pronounced 'dead mouse') name, inspired in part by finding the frozen remains of a rodent inside a computer. By the time he released his debut album, *Get Scraped*, in 2005, the mouse-head helmet had already become a feature of his performances.

Inspired by his music and intrigued by his elevation of DJing to a live spectacle, crowds flocked to his shows throughout the late 2000s. By the end of the decade, he was headlining festivals such as Sonar, Ultra Music and Lollapalooza, while his *4x4=12* album sold in huge quantities. By now, his shows were blurring the boundaries between DJing and live performance, while utilizing his legendary helmet to provide visual and lighting effects.

Deadmau5's position as dance music's biggest draw was confirmed in 2012, when he became the first electronic musician to be featured on the cover of American rock music magazine, *Rolling Stone*.

**Pioneer**

*Most of Deadmau5's public performances blur the boundaries between a DJ set and a live performance. To do this, he uses a combination of DJing, performance and studio equipment, with his now famous headgear adding a dazzling light show to enhance the experience for fans.*

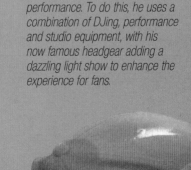

FAVOURED STYLES:

**EDM**
**ELECTRO-HOUSE**
**TECH-HOUSE**
**TECHNO**

# CHAPTER 4:

# ADVANCED MIXING TECHNIQUES

Once you have mastered the fundamentals of mixing, you can begin to look at more advanced techniques. Once you have perfected these, they will help you mix like a pro, while entertaining eager crowds of people.

**LEFT:** Qbert is one of the most talented DJs on the planet, capable of slinging together amazing routines full of cuts, scratches and turntable tricks. He also helped to design the revolutionary Vestax QFO turntable, which featured a built-in two-channel mixer.

# ADVANCED BEAT MATCHING

Keeping two records in time while simultaneously operating the mixer is tricky. Thankfully, there are a few tricks you can use to keep your mixes sounding tighter, for longer.

### KEEPING VINYL RECORDS IN TIME FOR LONGER

Direct drive turntables, such as Technics SL-1210s, rarely keep perfect time. They will waver in and out of time by tiny amounts, meaning that you will need to make minor adjustments to keep the beats synchronized. There are several ways of doing this.

#### • Riding the pitch

This involves using the turntables' pitch control faders to keep two songs locked in time. If you've got the drumbeats in time before starting the mix, you should only need to make subtle adjustments to the speed to keep the BPMs matched.

#### • Touching the platter

Lightly touching the side of the sloped edge of the platter with two fingers will momentarily slow it down a little. You can also perform this trick by pulling your fingers across the edge of the platter in a backwards movement. The first time you try it, you may slow the platter down too much. With practice, you'll become a pro.

#### • Touching the label

Some DJs prefer not to tweak the spindle to quickly speed up the record. Instead, they use a finger or two to manually push round the record. This is easiest if you do it closest to the centre of the record, as shown in the picture below.

#### • Tweaking the spindle (above)

You can momentarily speed up a record by tweaking the turntable's central spindle with your thumb and middle finger. Simply grasp it lightly and turn it clockwise. Getting it right takes practice, but after a while it will become natural.

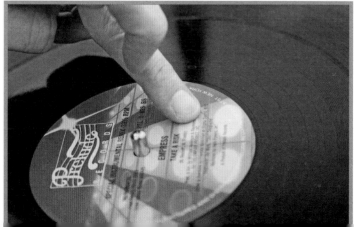

## KEEPING CD TURNTABLES IN TIME FOR LONGER

The digital nature of CD turntables means that they generally keep better time than vinyl decks. Even so, you'll still need to make adjustments to ensure your mixes are smooth and synchronized. As on vinyl decks, you can 'ride the pitch' using the turntables' pitch control faders. Some CD turntables also feature vinyl emulation, allowing you to use the jog dial to subtly speed up or slow down a track.

**1.** If you're using one of Pioneer's industry-standard CDJ models, turn it to 'vinyl' mode. To momentarily speed up a track, use two fingers to push the side of the jog dial forwards. You can adjust the sensitivity of the jog dial to suit whether you prefer a light or strong touch.

**2.** To slow down a song for a short period, simply use two fingers to lightly pull the edge of the jog dial towards you. Generally, you'll only need to use a light flick of the fingers.

# DIFFERENT MIXING STYLES

Once you've mastered keeping mixes in time for longer, you can start to focus more on your mixing style. Some DJs prefer overlaying different musical elements of songs in long blends, while others prefer the quick, energetic feel of cutting and scratching.

If you've tried keeping two songs in time for an extended period, you'll have noticed that not all of the different musical elements sound great together. Basslines, chords, melodies and vocals can all clash if the records aren't compatible, or are mixed together poorly.

## ADVANCED MIXER CONTROLS

You can get round this in a couple of ways. First, you can use the mixer's EQ controls to alter certain frequencies of each song during the mix. Turning the 'low' EQ right down,

**DJ Fresh (left)**
*Pioneering drum & bass producer DJ Fresh is renowned for his quick-mixing style, and performing sets that incorporate other styles such as EDM, electro-house, dubstep and hip-hop.*

**Eddie Halliwell (below)**
*Hard dance star Eddie Halliwell rose to fame with a DJ style that blended fast, energetic house and trance music with the scratches and turntable techniques more associated with hip-hop.*

for example, will significantly reduce the level of bass and the heaviness of the drumbeats, while the 'high' knob can be used to turn down cymbals and melodies. By learning to use these during the mix, you can improve the soundness and smoothness of your blends.

## MIXING IN KEY

Another more advanced way to guarantee great-sounding blends is to use harmonious mixing. That means mixing records that are in the same musical key, or keys that are compatible. The theory is rather complex, but you can tell when you've nailed a harmonious mix, as the musical elements of both songs sound good together. You can find lots of advice about how to mix harmoniously on the Internet, including video tutorials.

## CUTTING AND SCRATCHING

Some DJs, particularly those who play hip-hop and drum & bass, prefer to use a more energetic, fast-paced style of mixing. This combines the art of 'cutting' – using the crossfader to quickly jump between songs – and 'scratching'.

The latter is a collection of techniques that revolve around manipulating vinyl records by hand to create distinctive sounds. Collectively, DJs who use these techniques – and compete with each other at DJ battles – are known as turntablists.

Turntablism is an impressive art form in its own right. There are a large number of techniques that combine cutting and scratching. In the rest of this chapter, we'll show you how to perform some of them.

**Scratch Perverts**
*British trio Scratch Perverts are renowned for their energetic performances, which see them use between four and six turntables. By doing this, they can quickly switch between many musical styles, while also performing amazing scratches and turntable tricks.*

# YOUR FIRST SCRATCH

We'll start our scratching tutorials by looking at the most basic scratch of all, the baby scratch, and its big brother, the scribble. They are performed one-handed, using your fingers and wrist to move a record backwards and forwards.

Before you begin, take some time to find a sound you'd like to scratch on one of your records. Scratches can be performed with a drum sound, such as the first kick drum of a song, or a snare drum hit, or with other musical sounds. Collections of sounds suitable for scratching, known as battle records, are also available to buy.

Once you've found a sound you want to use, cue the record up at that point, and hold it in place with the middle fingers of one hand. The platter should be spinning below, the mixer crossfader set to the central position, and the channel faders pushed up.

### THE BABY SCRATCH

To perform the baby scratch, simply push the record forward with your fingers so that the sound plays, before pulling it back to the starting position. How does it sound? Try attempting the baby scratch at different speeds, to hear

**Open Faders (above)**
*Most turntablists keep both channel faders open during their sets. This means that both are pushed up, allowing them to control what the audience hears entirely using the crossfader. This way, they'll always have a hand free to scratch.*

**Flexible Fingers**
*Although some of the movement to perform the baby scratch comes from your wrist, it's the knuckles and fingers that do most of the work. If you're unsure about what you should be doing, there are plenty of great tutorials on video-sharing sites such as YouTube.*

the difference in sound. Most turntablists perform baby scratches quite quickly, though getting a smooth, speedy, great-sounding scratch takes time to perfect. You also need to be able to scratch with either hand, which doesn't always feel natural. In other words, get practising!

**Pushed Forward (above)**
*As you extend your fingers and perform the forward movement of the baby scratch, the palm of your hand will naturally move closer to the record. If it touches the platter, though, you're doing something wrong!*

**Draw Back (right)**
*Remember, the distinctive baby scratch sound comes not from simply pushing the record forward, but also by quickly pulling it back to the starting position.*

**DJ TIP:** Most turntablists prefer to scratch using vinyl turntables and records, but it is also possible to do it on some CD decks. You'll need a CDJ that features vinyl emulation. On those models, you can perform scratches using the jog dial. The techniques are exactly the same, though the feel of the dial's surface is naturally different to manipulating a record by hand.

## THE SCRIBBLE

The scribble is a more advanced version of the baby scratch, performed with the fingers closer together, and the arm held straighter and higher. The idea is to make smaller, quicker movements backwards and forwards, resulting in a shorter scratching sound. Performing good scribble scratches is harder than you think. Your hand, wrist and arm should be more rigid, with the movement – quick and slight – coming from your elbow. It will take time to perfect, so get stuck into some practice sooner rather than later!

### High Wrist
*Unlike the baby scratch, which is best performed by keeping your wrist and fingers relaxed, the scribble demands a rigid wrist and fingers. You should be attempting short, quick movements rather than the longer ones associated with the baby scratch.*

# THE FORWARD SCRATCH

The forward scratch is a perfect way to learn the art of simultaneously cutting and scratching. It is best performed as a cool effect while a song plays on the other turntable, in order to add something extra to your DJ performances.

The theory behind the forward scratch is simple. Despite the name, it's not really a scratch at all. The technique involves quickly playing and stopping a record, while simultaneously moving the crossfader from side to side. Turntablists usually perform it using short sounds (known as 'samples'), such as the 'aaah' and 'fresh' noises often heard in hip-hop mixtapes.

Before you begin, push up both of your mixer's channel faders, and set the crossfader to the opposite side to the turntable you'll be scratching on. Make sure your headphones are plugged in, and on your head – you'll need them.

**1.** Find and cue up the sound you wish to use, and hold the record in place with your fingers.

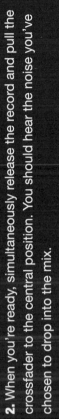

The theory behind the Forward Scratch is simple. Despite the name, it's not really a scratch at all. It involves quickly playing and stopping a record, while simultaneously moving the crossfader from side to side. Turntablists usually perform it using short sounds (known as 'samples'), such as the 'aaah' and 'fresh' noises often heard in hip-hop mix-tapes.

Before you begin, push up both of your mixer's channel faders, and set the crossfader to the opposite side to the turntable you'll be scratching on. Make sure your headphones are plugged in, and on your head – you'll need them.

**1.** Find and cue up the sound you wish to use, and hold the record in place with your fingers. With the other hand, hold the crossfader lightly between your thumb and forefinger.

**2.** When you're ready, simultaneously release the record and pull the crossfader to the central position. You should hear the noise you've chosen to drop into the mix.

**3.** As soon as the sound has played, quickly stop the record playing with your hand, and push the crossfader back to its original position.

**4.** Finally, pull the record back to its starting position so that you're ready to go again. You can find this point more easily using the mixer's PFL or cue buttons.

Through practice, you should get pretty nifty at dropping, stopping and rewinding the record, whilst quickly opening and closing the crossfader. Performing the forward scratch successfully is as much about co-ordination as mastering the specific skills involved.

4

3

# THE TRANSFORMER SCRATCH

**1**

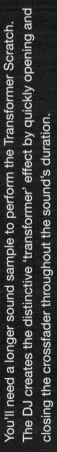

**2**

You'll need a longer sound sample to perform the Transformer Scratch. The DJ creates the distinctive 'transformer' effect by quickly opening and closing the crossfader throughout the sound's duration.

**1.** Select a nice, long sound or sample to practice with, and set the turntable's pitch control to its slowest setting. Next, set up the mixer and cue up the record as you would for a Forward Scratch. You should be holding the record in place with one hand, and holding the crossfader with the other.

**4**

**3**

**2.** Simultaneously release the record and open the crossfader by pulling it across to the central position.

**3.** Quickly close the crossfader by pushing it back to its original position.

**4.** Repeat this opening and closing motion for the duration of the sample. The quicker you do it, the better the effect. As with the forward scratch, stop the record with your fingers the moment the sound you're playing is complete. As with all scratches, the Transformer Scratch takes time to perfect, so practice regularly.

# SCRATCHING

## BABY SCRATCH

Scratches can be performed with a drum sound, such as the first kick drum of a song, or a snare drum hit, or with other musical sounds. Collections of sounds for scratching, known as battle records, are also available to buy.

Once you've found a sound you want to use, cue the record up at that point, and hold it in place with your middle fingers. The platter should be spinning below, the mixer crossfader set to the central position, and the channel faders pushed up.

To perform the baby scratch, push the record forward with your fingers so that the sound plays, before pulling it back to the starting position. How does it sound? Try attempting the baby scratch at different speeds, to hear the difference in sound. Most turntablists perform baby scratches quite quickly, though getting a smooth, speedy, great-sounding scratch takes time to perfect. You also need to be able to scratch with either hand, which doesn't always feel natural. In other words, get practising!

### Flexible Fingers

*Although some of the movement to perform the baby scratch comes from your wrist, it's the knuckles and fingers that do most of the work. If you're still unsure about what you should be doing, there are plenty of great tutorial films on video sharing sites such as YouTube.*

### Draw Back

*Remember, the distinctive baby scratch sound comes not from simply pushing the*

### Open Faders

*Most turntablists keep both channel faders open during their sets. This means that both are pushed up, allowing them to control what the audience hears entirely using the crossfader. This way, they'll always have a hand free to scratch.*

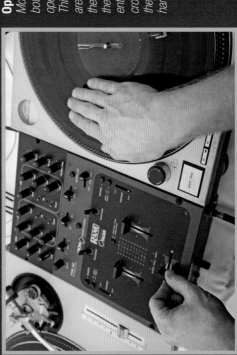

### Pushed Forward

*As you extend your fingers and perform the forward movement of the baby scratch, the*

...sound forward, but also by quickly pulling it back to the starting position.

...palm of your hand will naturally move closer to the record. If it touches the platter, though, you're doing something wrong!

# SCRIBBLE SCRATCH

The Scribble is a more advanced version of the baby scratch, performed with the fingers closer together, and the arm held straighter and higher. The idea is to make smaller, quicker movements backwards and forwards, resulting in a shorter scratching sound. Performing good Scribble scratches is harder than you think. Your hand, wrist and arm should be more rigid, with the movement – quick and slight – coming from your elbow. It will take time to perfect, so get stuck into some practice sooner rather than later!

### High Wrist

*Unlike the baby scratch, which is best performed by keeping your wrist and fingers relaxed, the scribble demands a rigid wrist and fingers. You should be attempting short, quick movements, rather than the longer ones associated with the baby scratch.*

# THE FORWARD SCRATCH

2

1

**2.** With the other hand, hold the crossfader lightly between your thumb and forefinger.

**3.** When you're ready, simultaneously release the record and pull the crossfader to the central position. You should hear the noise you've chosen to drop into the mix. As soon as the sound has played, quickly stop the record playing with your hand, and push the crossfader back to its original position.

**4.** Finally, pull the record back to its starting position so that you're ready to go again. You can find this point more easily using the mixer's PFL or cue buttons.

Through practice, you should get pretty nifty at dropping, stopping and rewinding the record, while quickly opening and closing the crossfader. Performing the forward scratch successfully is as much about co-ordination as mastering the specific skills involved.

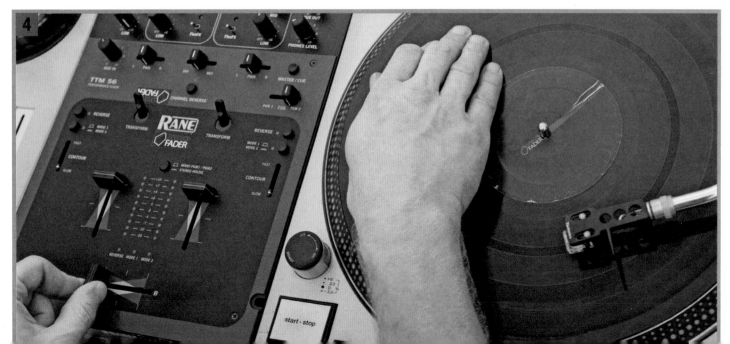

# THE TRANSFORMER SCRATCH

The transformer scratch is a little like the forward scratch. It was invented by a trio of DJs in the 1980s, and was named after the sound made by a 'transforming' robot in the *Transformers* cartoon series.

You'll need a longer sound sample to perform the transformer scratch. The DJ creates the distinctive 'transformer' effect by quickly opening and closing the crossfader throughout the sound's duration.

**1.** Select a nice, long sound or sample to practise with, and set the turntable's pitch control to its slowest setting. Next, set up the mixer and cue up the record as you would for a forward scratch. You should be holding the record in place with one hand, and holding the crossfader with the other.

**2.** Simultaneously release the record and open the crossfader by pulling it across to the central position.

**3.** Quickly close the crossfader by pushing it back to its original position.

**4.** Repeat this opening and closing motion for the duration of the sample. The quicker you do it, the better the effect. As with the forward scratch, stop the record with your fingers the moment the sound you're playing is complete. As with all scratches, the transformer scratch takes time to perfect, so practise it regularly.

**DJ TIP:** To make it easier to find the start points of their favourite samples, many turntablists place stickers on their battle records. These stickers are used to mark the exact place on the record that the sample begins. This way, they can re-set the record by eye, without needing to use headphones.

# GRANDMASTER FLASH

## 1958–

### RECOMMENDED LISTENING:

*The Adventures of Grandmaster Flash On The Wheels Of Steel* (single, 1981)

*Essential Mix: Classics Edition* (DJ mix CD, 2002)

During the early years of hip-hop, Grandmaster Flash did more than any other DJ to popularize cutting and scratching. He even invented a number of techniques that are now considered standard skills among hip-hop DJs.

Born Joseph Saddler in Barbados, but raised in the Bronx area of New York, Flash began DJing as a teenager and quickly learnt to replicate the techniques of trail-blazing local DJs such as DJ Kool Herc, Grandmaster Flowers and Grand Wizzard Theodore.

Flash became a sensation on the New York block party scene after unveiling his own pioneering DJ technique: quick-mix theory. This involved creating extended drum loops by quickly flicking between two copies of the same record. The technique remains popular to this day, and is sometimes referred to as 'beat juggling'.

Having perfected early hip-hop mixing, he began his recording career alongside rap crew The Furious Five in 1979. They went on to be hugely successful worldwide, hitting the pop charts with hip-hop and electro classics such as 'The Message' and 'White Lines (Don't Do It)'.

Flash's most significant release remains 1981's 'The Adventures of Grandmaster Flash On The Wheels Of Steel' – a seven-minute mash-up of samples, sounds and drum loops created using two turntables, a mixer and a pile of records. It was the first record to effectively capture a DJ performance.

**Crowd Pleaser**
*Grandmaster Flash continues to draw crowds wherever he plays, almost 40 years after he first took to the turntables in his bedroom in the Bronx, New York.*

FAVOURED STYLES:

**HIP-HOP**
**DISCO**
**FUNK & SOUL**
**ELECTRO**

# CHAPTER 5:
# COMPUTER DJING

The rise of the 'laptop DJ' has been one of the biggest developments seen in DJing over the last decade. Thanks to groundbreaking computer software, DJs can deliver more creative performances than ever before.

LEFT: Pete Tong began his DJ career in the 1980s, playing vinyl-only sets. Today, he uses a laptop with Traktor Pro and two MIDI controllers, allowing him to create more inventive performances.

# BLURRING THE BOUNDARIES

Once, DJing was the sole preserve of obsessive music collectors, who spent huge amounts of money on vinyl records. Today, specialist computer software puts DJing in the hands of anyone with a laptop computer and a bunch of cheap MP3 files.

The digital DJ revolution began in 2001, when techno DJs Richie Hawtin and John Acquaviva began testing a revolutionary new system called Final Scratch. Developed by a Dutch software company, it allowed the duo to play music stored on a laptop computer, using two turntables, special 'control vinyl' records and an audio interface. It was the first digital vinyl system (DVS), and it effectively heralded a new era in DJing.

## LIMITLESS POTENTIAL

The software program at the heart of today's DVS packages, such as Traktor Pro (the replacement for Final Scratch) and Serato DJ, is designed to offer many more features than DJs have come to expect from traditional hardware. These options – sample banks, cue points, sound effects, loops, even options for the software to mix the tracks for you – allow DJs to unleash their creativity.

**Amon Tobin**
*During his 2003 tour, Amon Tobin became one of the first DJs to use Final Scratch, the world's first DVS package. One of his shows from the tour was released as a mix CD.*

**The Orb (2014)**
*Ambient house pioneers, The Orb, combine the manipulation of grooves using Ableton Live performance software and live mixing of song elements using two Pioneer CDJ-2000s.*

## MAKING SENSE OF SOFTWARE

Today, it is this software, rather than the ability to control it using vinyl or CD turntables, that is at the heart of laptop DJing. It is now possible to mix using the computer keyboard, plug-in DVS interfaces or dedicated DJ controller hardware. Should a DJ so wish, he or she can even buy the individual musical elements that make up their favourite dance tracks (known as 'stems'), and mix new versions of these songs using their favourite software package. Sometimes, these performances are created using MIDI controllers originally designed for music production, rather than DJing.

This blurring of the boundaries between DJing and live performance, combined with the sheer volume of different control options, can be overwhelming for beginners. In the rest of this chapter, we'll try to help you make sense of computer DJing.

## HOW DVS WORKS

Digital vinyl systems, sometimes called vinyl emulation, allow DJs to perform sets with digital audio files, such as MP3s, as they would with regular turntables. The 'timecode' vinyl records or CDs, which are used to 'play' audio files stored on the DJ's laptop computer, contain digital information that the software uses to determine any changes in playback speed and direction. The DVS audio interface routes this information to the software, which then returns it to the mixer as sound. DJs feel as if they're playing regular records or CDs, and can perform as they would with the equipment associated with those formats.

# UNIQUE FUNCTIONS

Every DJing software package is slightly different, but they share a number of features and tools to enable creative DJing. Here, we outline some of the most popular functions, and what you can do with them.

Although there are now countless programs to choose from, DJ software packages generally feature a similar layout. Open up Serato DJ, Traktor Pro, Mixx or Virtual DJ, and you will see two virtual decks. It is into these that songs are loaded, ready to be mixed together. Each virtual deck features a display containing important information about the loaded song, including its duration and tempo (in beats per minute).

## WATCH THE WAVES

In many programs, you will also find a visual representation of the song as a waveform display. As a song plays, the waveform will move with it, keeping track of progress. These waveforms can also be used as a visual aid during mixing; if the tall lines of the displays by both virtual decks are in sync, then the beats match.

## CREATIVE TOOLS

Popular creative features regularly found in DJ software programs include:

### Loops

Many programs allow you to loop up short sections of songs, such as drum patterns, for use during mixing. It is usually possible to set up and save these loops beforehand, although you can also create them on the fly during performances.

### Cue Points

These can be used to quickly find the point from which you want to start playing a track. Setting a number of cue points throughout a song allows you the option to play only a small

**PCDJ (right)**
*Features of the Red Mobile version of PCDJ include a 'mix now' option, which automatically cross-fades between tracks playing on each of the virtual turntables.*

**Traktor Scratch Pro (left)**
*Unlike some other DJ software packages, Traktor Scratch Pro contains built-in mixer controls, as well as virtual turntables.*

## Virtual DJ

*Registered users of Virtual DJ, one of the most popular DJing software programs around, have access to a huge online library of music. As long as the DJ is connected to the Internet, he or she can play any of these songs in their performances.*

section, begin mixing the track midway through, or jump between different parts using the laptop's keyboard.

## Sound Effects

Add cool noises and audio effects to jazz up your mixes at the touch of a button.

## Sample Banks

Load up your own samples – noises, sounds, snippets of dialogue from films and TV shows – and spin them into the mix at any point you choose.

## Sync

Some packages feature 'sync' functions. When turned on, the software will mix tracks together for you.

## Flexibility

*DVS packages are particularly popular with scratch DJs, who enjoy the ability to easily cut between two copies of the same song.*

# DJ CONTROLLERS

Although it is possible to mix on most DJ software programs using just your laptop's keyboard, it is not a very fun experience. It is for this reason that manufacturers have developed dedicated DJ controllers for laptop DJs.

As the name suggests, a DJ controller is a piece of equipment designed to allow DJs to get the most from their DJ software. There are a large number of different designs and models available, but the vast majority of controllers boast the following key features:

• Crossfaders and upfaders on which to mix songs loaded onto the software's virtual decks.
• CD turntable-style control buttons (play, pause, track select, etc).
• Pads to trigger popular features such as cue points, loops and sound effects.
• Knobs to use as mixer-style EQs, or to help control sound effects.

**Traktor Kontrol S5**
*This controller, manufactured by Native Instruments, was designed to get the most out of Traktor Scratch Pro software. The faders, knobs and buttons exactly match those contained in the program.*

**Numark Mixdeck**
*With simple controls, large jog dials and numerous CDJ-style functions, Numark's Mixdeck 3 controller is one of the most popular options for those new to DJing.*

## HANDS-ON CONTROL

Many controllers also feature CD turntable-style jog dials, which can be used in a similar way during the mixing process. These help to give a more hands-on feel during mixing. These controllers tend to be bigger and, arguably, slightly bulkier. This means that they can be more awkward to use in smaller DJ booths – a surprisingly regular sight in bars and clubs – even if they are often easier to use.

Whatever model you choose, DJ controllers can be set up to suit the software you've chosen. Like MIDI controllers designed for music production, each controller's buttons, pads, knobs and faders can be assigned to specific software features using a process called mapping. You can find out more about the process online, and in the documentation that comes with DJ software programs.

## SIMPLE CONNECTION

One of the joys of DJ controllers is their all-in-one nature. By using the included mixer controls, you will never need to touch your DJ mixer (or the club's) for the duration of your performance. Simply plug the controller into one channel using audio leads, turn the fader up, and get on with it.

# MIDI CONTROLLERS

Some DJ software programs can also be operated using a MIDI controller. These are primarily designed for use with music production software, but can be a great option for those who wish to blur the boundaries between DJing and live performance.

Unless you have previously made electronic music, you may not be aware of MIDI. It's short for Musical Instrument Digital Interface, a technological standard that allows communication between electronic instruments, control devices and a computer. In music production, a MIDI controller can be used to operate software, play music and program beats. It can also be used as a performance tool, allowing a musician control over pre-recorded elements such as drum loops, chords and melodies.

## MIDI CONTROL FOR DJS

Because of their links to music production, most MIDI controllers do not feature DJ-specific features such as jog dials, crossfaders and so on. Some are designed to look like small mixing desks, with numerous channels (each with its own fader), to which individual elements of a track can be assigned. Others simply feature a mixture of pads, buttons and knobs with which to control the software.

Despite the lack of DJ-style mixing tools, many MIDI controllers work with DJ software. Users simply assign software functions to the buttons, pads and knobs using the mapping system discussed on the previous page.

**Pioneer DDJ-SP1**
*The Pioneer DDJ-SP1 MIDI controller was designed with Serato DJ in mind. Its pads, buttons and knobs can be used to control the software's cue points, sample banks and sound effects. It can also be used to create live edits of songs during performances.*

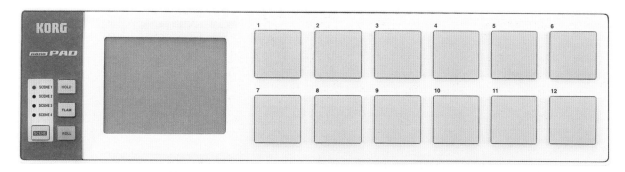

**Korg NanoPad (left)**

*The Korg NanoPad features a bank of pads that can be mapped to control certain functions in DJ software programs. These include setting and triggering cue points, and creating loops of drum patterns contained in the songs you're playing.*

## GOING LIVE!

MIDI controllers are arguably best suited to dual-purpose production and performance software, such as Ableton Live. These programs allow you to strip songs back to their constituent parts – or, of course, make your own – before creating and performing unique versions of them on the spot. MIDI controllers are perfect for this purpose. At the touch of a button, turn of a knob or tap of a pad, you can trigger loops, add special effects or bring new sounds in and out of the mix.

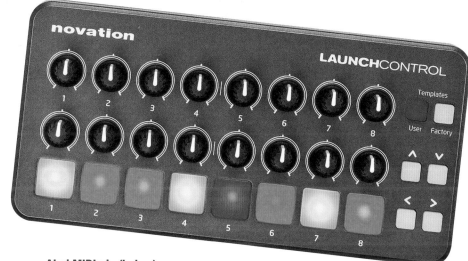

**Akai MIDImix (below)**

*The MIDImix is a great example of a MIDI controller that can be used for DJing, live performance and music production. It is modelled on portable mixing desks, most often used by bedroom producers.*

**Novation Launch Control (above)**

*This MIDI controller is made up of a mixture of buttons and knobs, which can be used to control specific aspects of DJing software packages. It is arguably better suited to the Ableton Live performance software, and is sold bundled with a version of the program.*

## DJ FRIENDLY?

If you are thinking of buying a MIDI controller, spend some time researching the features, functions and usability of any models you're considering. You need to find out whether the controller you are keen on is DJ software-friendly, as not all are. The mapping process can sometimes be tricky, too, so try to select one that can be set up and mapped quickly.

# DJ HEROES

# RICHIE HAWTIN

## 1970–

RECOMMENDED LISTENING:
*Decks, FX & 909* (DJ mix, 1999)
*DE9: Transitions* (DJ mix, 2005)

Since he first broke through in the early 1990s, English-born Canadian Richie Hawtin has thrilled in blurring the boundaries between DJing, live performance and music production.

Hawtin first found fame as a music producer, releasing brutal fusions of acid house and techno on the Plus8 label that he set up with fellow Canadian John Acquaviva. During this period, he began to introduce elements of live performance to his DJ appearances, using drum machines and other electronic hardware. This unique approach was captured for posterity on the groundbreaking 1999 DJ mix CD, *Decks, FX & 909*.

Hawtin continued to push forwards DJ and electronic

**Caption**
*Proin molestie diam vitae consequat placerat. Mauris tincidunt posuere tellus id feugiat. In quis sapien turpis. Maecenas vel mi interdum, fermentum*

music performance technology in the early part of the 21st century. He was involved with the development of the pioneering DVS product Final Scratch and its successor, Traktor DJ Pro. His enthusiasm stemmed from the system's creative potential, and his ability to use it to create performances that went far beyond the traditional confines of DJing. To prove a point, he used Final Scratch to brilliantly mash up and remix an impressive array of records on the 2003 mix album *DE9: Closer to the Edit.*

Predictably, Hawtin was also an early advocate of the Ableton Live performance software. This made it easier for him to combine elements of different tracks – both his own productions, and those by others – in unique ways during DJ gigs. As he'd previously done with his other pioneering performance projects, he put together a showcase mix CD, 2005's *DE9: Transitions.*

## FAVOURED STYLES:

## TECHNO
## MINIMAL TECHNO
## ACID HOUSE

### Lengthy Service
*In 2015, Hawtin released a surprise album called* From My Mind To Yours. *Designed to mark his 25th year in music production, the set contained tracks from his many projects, including Plastikman, FUSE and Circuit Breaker.*

# PERFORMANCE SOFTWARE

Richie Hawtin is just one of an increasing number of DJs to embrace performance software. These unique programs blur the boundaries between DJing, music production and live performance, allowing users to create sets that simply wouldn't be possible using traditional DJ equipment.

**Ableton Live**
*The performance screen of Ableton Live is designed to look like a virtual mixing desk. Elements of songs, such as drumbeats, basslines or melodies, can be dropped into each virtual channel, before being mixed and manipulated in real time.*

Imagine being able to quickly remix your favourite songs during a DJ set, before overlaying new drums and blending this with elements taken from a number of different tracks. Once you've done that, you could move onto layering up a number of different tracks at the same time, all of which remain firmly in time.

This scenario may seem a little futuristic and far-fetched, but it is perfectly possible with the world's leading dual-purpose music performance and production software: Ableton Live.

## PERFORMANCE AND PRODUCTION

Ableton Live is perhaps not the easiest option for new DJs, but it does open up many new avenues for creative DJing. Although it can be used to simply mix songs together, it doesn't look or feel like traditional DJing. For starters, the software's control screen looks more like something you'd find in a music production program. That's because Ableton Live can also be used to produce music, and it's this blurring of boundaries between music making, live performance and DJing that makes it such a powerful tool.

**Armin van Buuren**
*The world-famous Dutch trance DJ Armin van Buuren was an early adopter of Ableton Live, first using it to produce, perform and mix his* State of Trance *radio show. Today, he uses the software to produce tracks, perform them live, and sometimes to do DJ sets.*

## ON-SCREEN MIXING

Using Ableton Live, DJs can load up any number of songs, drum loops or musical elements, and mix them together in any way they like. The software contains an in-built mixer screen for this exact purpose. Anything you put into it will stay in time – meaning there's no tricky beat matching to perform – thanks to a clever innovation called warping. Once you have set a master tempo for your performance (120 BPM, for example), anything you decide to perform with will be 'warped' to fit this tempo, whatever its original speed.

**Skrillex**
*EDM/dubstep artist Skrillex is renowned for performing quick-fire DJ sets that change rapidly. He does this by using Ableton Live performance software to mash up elements from many different songs.*

# AUDIO-VISUAL

If simply mixing music together isn't enough to get the juices flowing, why not throw video into the mix as well? This is known as A/V DJing, and it is possible thanks to add-ons for popular DJ software programs.

**Pioneer DVJ-1000**
*When it was launched, Pioneer's DVJ-1000 was a landmark piece of equipment. Based on their popular CDJ-1000 turntable, it allowed DJs to manipulate and mix DVDs for the first time. Unfortunately, it was also hugely expensive to buy, putting it beyond the reach of all but the most dedicated A/V DJs.*

**Hexstatic (right)**
*A/V DJ duo Hexstatic first began mixing audio and visuals live in clubs in the 1990s, making them pioneers. They are famous for creating audio-visual tracks that contain sounds and elements sampled from film footage. Their albums are normally released in both audio and video formats.*

Once upon a time, video mixing was a long-winded and highly complicated affair. In the 1990s and early 2000s, it was the preserve of specialist 'VJs', who mixed with expensive, bulky equipment. These days, though, it is possible using a laptop, regular DJ software and homemade video clips, making it accessible even to bedroom DJs.

## SYNCHRONICITY

Of course, that's not to say that video mixing is the easiest thing for beginners to get into. Not only do you need to build up an extensive music collection, but also a similarly large selection of videos. These clips will also need to be synchronized with the music you're playing, either using the video mixing plug-ins available for some popular DJ software packages, or an entirely separate software package, such as GrandVJ. You will also need to buy a projector, and the leads to plug it into your laptop. If you also use DVS as your preferred control method, this means you will need to take a lot of equipment with you when you go out to DJ.

## VIDEO KILLED THE RADIO STAR

There are benefits to A/V DJing, though, not least the ability to stand out from the crowd. DJs such as Hexstatic, Coldcut and DJ Cheeba have all become famous for their dedication to blending music and video during their sets, while trance legend Armin van Buuren has also dabbled in the world of A/V mixing. It's a lot easier to get into than it once was, with Serato DJ, MixVibes and Virtual DJ all offering video mixing plug-ins. If it's something that interests you, read up on it online before making a decision.

# CHAPTER 6:

# FINDING YOUR STYLE

We've talked about equipment, DJ techniques and laptop mixing. Now it's time to focus on music, to help you develop your own unique DJ style.

**LEFT:** Ben UFO is one of the most in-demand DJs on the underground, thanks to an open-minded style that takes in such diverse styles as techno, dubstep, house, electronica, UK funky and drum & bass.

# STANDING OUT

There's more to being a great DJ than tight mixing skills. What music you play, and when, is arguably much more important. By creating this musical identity, you can develop a DJ style all of your own.

Listen to recordings of high-profile DJs at work, and you'll notice significant differences in the tracks they select, and the ways in which they choose to play them. Take techno DJs Jeff Mills and Ricardo Villalobos as examples; while the former is known for quickly mixing between short loops of funky, fast records, the latter prefers playing tracks for longer, creating hypnotic blends of minimal-sounding records. Both are techno DJs, but their styles couldn't be more different.

## TIME AND DEDICATION

So how do you develop a DJ style? For starters, it takes time. The best DJs hone their craft over a number of years. During that time, they will amass a large music collection, which they know inside out. Through trial and error, and watching the reaction of dancers, they will work out the best ways to select and mix together those records, CDs or MP3s.

## KNOWLEDGE IS POWER

If you've come this far, it's likely that there is a particular style, or styles, of music that you are most keen on playing. This is a good start. However, do you know the roots of that style, how it developed, and the sub-genres – basically the styles within styles – associated with it? Similarly, how well do you understand other forms of dance music, and how they are related? When it comes to music, knowledge really is power.

In this chapter, we're going to look at popular dance music styles in detail, focusing on key stylistic traits, and how DJs choose to play them. In 20 pages' time, you should be a bit clearer on where you want to go as a DJ.

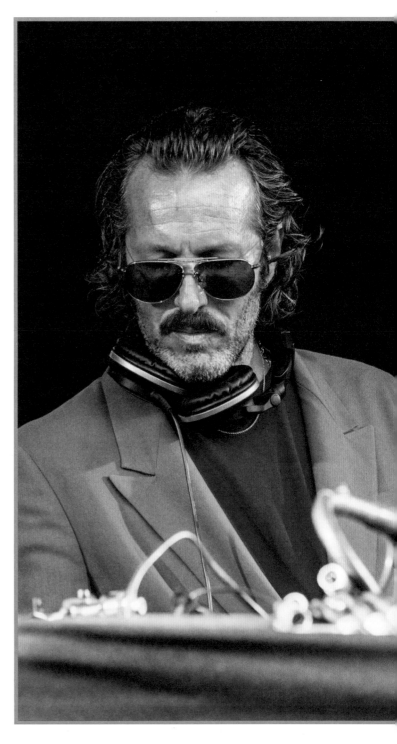

**DJ Harvey**
*Over the course of 25 years, DJ Harvey has become renowned for the obscurity of the songs he plays, and for his ability to play long sets that include a wide variety of musical styles.*

**Jeff Mills**
*The Detroit legend is famed for the energetic nature of his sets, an effect created by quickly mixing between short loops of fast and funky techno tracks.*

**DJ Marky**
*The Brazilian selector peps up his party-friendly drum & bass sets with the kind of amazing scratching routines normally associated with hip-hop DJs.*

# DISCO

The roots of most modern dance music, and DJ culture itself, can be traced back to disco. In the 21st century, it's undergoing a renaissance, too.

Disco emerged in New York in the 1970s, and took the world by storm. The people who originally played it, such as Nicky Siano, Walter Gibbons, François Kevorkian and Larry Levan, were arguably the first superstar DJs. They were pioneers, too, developing the beat-matching style of mixing.

Original disco records were fun, upbeat and characterized by heavy, dancefloor-friendly rhythms. Most 1970s and early 1980s disco records feature live drums, making them harder to mix. Because of this, classic disco songs are often mixed together quickly.

Today, disco is back. Nu-disco, which features more electronic drums and instruments, has been popular since the early 2000s, and shares some stylistic traits with house.

## TEMPO RANGE
110–130 BPM

## SUB-GENRES
Boogie, Italo-disco, nu-disco, cosmic disco

## RELATED STYLES
Funk, soul, house

**Larry Levan**
*After championing disco, Larry Levan helped pioneer a soulful, electronic form of house music that would become known as 'garage'.*

# HOUSE

Since the mid-1980s, house, and its many sub-genres, has dominated dancefloors. House is the spiritual heir to disco and often features similar drum patterns.

House music was developed in Chicago in the mid-1980s. Early house productions were heavily influenced by disco and European new-wave electronic pop music, and were created using electronic instruments and drum machines.

House music has since gone in many different directions, spawning a large number of sub-genres. These vary from tech-house (influenced by the futuristic sounds of techno) and soulful house (notable for the prominent use of vocals),

to acid house (intense and heavily electronic) and tribal house (dense, heavily percussive).

Some DJs specialize in one sub-genre, while others enjoy playing a broad range of house tracks. House music lends itself to a number of mixing styles, including quick transitions, long blends and harmonious mixes.

## TEMPO RANGE
118–128 BPM

## SUB-GENRES
Acid house, deep house, tech-house, soulful house, progressive house, electro house

## RELATED STYLES
Disco, boogie, US garage, techno

**Maya Jane Coles**
*Since breaking through in the late 2000s, British DJ Maya Jane Coles has become known for blurring the boundaries between deep house, tech-house and techno.*

# TECHNO

Like house, techno is built around repetitive, four-to-the-floor drumbeats. Although traditionally faster than house, the two styles are often mixed together.

Since coming out of Detroit in the mid-1980s, techno has become one of the most popular forms of dance music. Although it was initially futuristic in outlook, blending spacey synthesizers with repetitive kick-drum sounds, it has since spawned a number of sub-genres. These include the more sparse and hypnotic minimal techno, and the more musically varied intelligent techno.

Techno tracks often feature faster, heavier beats and

fewer musical elements than you'd find in house music. Some techno styles lend themselves to energetic mixing styles, while others are perfect for long, drawn-out blends.

**TEMPO RANGE**
125–140 BPM

**SUB-GENRES**
Dub techno, minimal techno, Detroit techno, acid techno, intelligent techno

**RELATED STYLES**
Tech-house, electro, acid house

**Kraftwerk**
*The German band Kraftwerk pioneered a brand of hypnotic, repetitive electronic music made with synthesizers and drum machines during the 1970s and 1980s. This inspired a group of DJs in Detroit, who created the blueprint for what would become techno music.*

# TRANCE

Trance is one of the most popular dance music styles in the world, with top DJs regularly playing to crowds of thousands.

**Above & Beyond**
*Through their DJ sets, productions and the releases on their Anjunabeats label, Above & Beyond have pushed variants of trance music that emphasize deeper and more melodic musical elements.*

## TEMPO RANGE
125–150 BPM

## SUB-GENRES
Psy-trance, progressive trance, uplifting trance, hard trance, tech-trance

## RELATED STYLES
Hard house, hardstyle, techno

When Trance was first recognized as a style of dance music in the 1990s, it shared some similarities with progressive house and techno. Now, the sound is more rigidly defined, and forms a musical movement in its own right.

Trance records are characterized by fast, heavy beats and the use of repetitive musical motifs. Tracks usually build up over a few minutes, before dropping into a beatless 'breakdown'. The beats will then be reintroduced and the track will build towards a climax. This 'build and release' format is hugely popular with dancers, and is designed to create excitement. It is for this reason that trance is often described as 'euphoric'.

# PAUL VAN DYK

## 1971–

**RECOMMENDED LISTENING:**
*Seven Ways* (album, 1996)
*Global* (DJ mix, 2002)

No other DJ or producer has done more for trance music than Paul van Dyk. During the early to mid-1990s, his tracks, remixes and albums effectively defined the sound, guaranteeing him legendary status within dance music. Readers of *DJ* magazine have twice voted him the World's Number One DJ.

Van Dyk began his DJ career in 1991, becoming a fixture at legendary Berlin techno club Tresor. It was when he began making and releasing music, though, that he really began to alter dance music for good.

Throughout 1993 and 1994, van Dyk put out a number of EPs that showcased a new take on techno. More hypnotic and trippy with bolder melody lines, greater use of sharp synthesizer lines and extended, beat-less breakdowns, the style was soon christened 'trance'. The German DJ/producer defined the sound further on the 1996 album *Seven Ways*, which is now considered a trance classic.

As the 1990s progressed, a number of his tracks, including 'For An Angel', 'Words', 'Beautiful Place' and 'Flaming June' (co-produced with BT), became huge worldwide dancefloor hits. Van Dyk was subsequently asked to become a resident DJ at leading UK superclub Gatecrasher.

By the early 2000s, van Dyk was one of the world's most in-demand DJs. He toured the world, playing in massive venues, and released mix CDs that sold in huge numbers. Nearly 25 years after he first took to the decks, van Dyk remains one of the most revered and celebrated DJs on the planet.

# TECH-TRANCE
# PROGRESSIVE
# TRANCE
# TECHNO

## Blurring Boundaries

*Paul van Dyk continues to be a pioneer, some 25 years after defining the sound of trance. Now, he blurs the boundaries between DJing and live performance during his sets at clubs and festivals around the world.*

# DRUM & BASS

Drum & bass is one of the most energetic styles of dance music, notable for its use of heavy bass and complex drum patterns.

What we now call drum & bass was initially known as jungle music. It was born in the early 1990s as a faster and more bass-heavy alternative to hardcore rave music. It has since become much more musically diverse, with sub-genres that are variously influenced by techno, soul, jazz and reggae.

While house, techno and trance tracks arrange

drumbeats in a straightforward 'four to the floor' pattern, drum & bass is built around speeded-up breakbeats. These are more varied rhythmically, with sequences of kick and snare drums that mimic the playing of drummers on old jazz and funk records.

Most drum & bass DJs tend to mix quickly, frequently moving between different tracks in order to keep energy levels high. Some are also keen turntablists and, like hip-hop DJs, perform in clubs alongside rappers (known as 'MCs').

## TEMPO RANGE
150–180 BPM

## SUB-GENRES
Tech-step, dark D&B, liquid D&B, jungle, jump-up

## RELATED STYLES
Dubstep, hip-hop, breaks

**Grooverider**
*During the early 1990s, Grooverider and long-time DJ partner Fabio played a pivotal role in the development of jungle and drum & bass.*

# DUBSTEP

Thanks to DJs such as Skrillex and Skream, the bass-heavy style of dubstep is now one of the most popular styles of dance music on the planet.

Compared to some of the genres we have discussed, dubstep is a relatively recent development. It emerged from the British cities of London and Bristol in the early 2000s, with pioneering producers fusing elements of drum & bass, UK garage and dub reggae.

Dubstep tracks are characterized by the sparseness of their sound. The sound's power is derived from the use of long, deep bass sounds, which are sometimes designed to feel as if they're 'wobbling'. Dubstep beat patterns vary, but typically feature a series of kick drums followed by a snare.

Traditionally, dubstep music is quite deep, heavy and atmospheric, though top DJs such as Skrillex and Skream often play angrier, more aggressive-sounding tracks.

**Skream**
*Although he now plays just as much disco and EDM, Skream will always be associated with dubstep. He was arguably the style's first superstar DJ.*

## TEMPO RANGE
**135–145 BPM**

## SUB-GENRES
**Breakstep, post-dubstep**

## RELATED STYLES
**Trap, UK garage, grime, drum & bass, broken beat, bass music**

# HIP-HOP

Hip-hop, sometimes called rap music, was one of the first styles of music to develop from DJ culture.

In the late 1970s, some New York DJs began looping up short sections of songs using two copies of the same record in order to entertain dancers. Rappers started to talk rhythmically over the top of their performances, and hip-hop was born.

Hip-hop tracks tend to be based around looped-up chunks of previously released songs, known as samples. Classic hip-hop records often feature samples of drumbeats and musical grooves taken from soul, funk and disco records.

The style of DJing most associated with hip-hop is turntablism. Hip-hop DJs tend to cut, scratch and mix quickly. Tracks vary in speed, but tend to be fairly slow. This means that they can easily be mixed with reggae, or the original soul, funk and disco records they sample.

## TEMPO RANGE
90–120 BPM

## SUB-GENRES
Electro, crunk, gangsta rap, hip-house, glitch hop, experimental hip-hop, trip-hop

## RELATED STYLES
Grime, drum & bass, reggae, breakbeat, disco, funk, soul

**Beastie Boys**
During the 1980s, the Beastie Boys played an important role in popularizing hip-hop. They made rap music accessible to rock fans by including heavy guitars in their tracks, before going on to create some of the greatest hip-hop records of all time.

# REGGAE

Reggae is one of the slowest styles of dance music around, but also one of the heaviest.

Reggae was the first style of dance music to emphasize the rhythm underpinning the song. The music is characterized by prominent basslines, slow but heavy drum patterns, and guitar riffs that appear in the space between the beats (known as the 'offbeat').

Reggae's sparser, heavier big brother is known as dub. Tracks in the dub style are usually instrumental, and make extensive use of special effects such as echo, reverb and delay. The influence of dub can be heard in many styles of dance music, including jungle, drum & bass, hip-hop and dubstep. There are also dub-influenced variants of house and techno.

Many reggae DJs think of themselves as 'selectors'. This is because they often select and sequence records, playing songs one after the other, rather than beat matching them.

## TEMPO RANGE
60–100 BPM

## SUB-GENRES
Dub reggae, roots reggae, lovers' rock, ragga, dancehall

## RELATED STYLES
Hip-hop, jungle, drum & bass, dub disco, dub house, dub techno, calypso, ska

**Reggae Sound System**
*Reggae can trace its roots back to Jamaica, where the music would be played by DJs on mobile sound systems. The DJs would talk, or 'toast', over the music, which explains why many reggae records feature instrumental B-sides with no singing.*

# JOINING THE DOTS

There is no rule saying that DJs should stick to one sound or style. Although many do, others prefer to select the best tracks from different genres and play them together in the same DJ set.

There is nothing new about DJs 'joining the dots' between different styles. In fact, during the 1980s, most DJs played a broad range of sounds in their sets. Even though many DJs now choose to focus on a particular genre, lots of famous names – including Jackmaster, Mr Scruff, Gilles Peterson, Ben UFO, Laurent Garnier and Annie Mac – owe their success to this kind of eclectic approach.

## DIFFERENT STROKES FOR DIFFERENT FOLKS

Some styles of dance music are frequently played together, such as disco, house and techno, or dubstep, drum & bass and hip-hop. This is partly because they share similar characteristics, such as tempo range and drum patterns, but also because of their history. For example, the DJs and musicians who made the first house records had previously been playing disco and boogie.

> **DJ TIP:** DVS software programs make it easier to move between styles. Users can arrange the tracks in their music library by tempo, while the virtual decks' waveform displays make it easier to match up different types of drumbeats.

**Annie Mac (below)**
*Dancers respond enthusiastically to Irish DJ Annie Mac's wide-ranging sets, which, like her radio show, include the best dance music from a wide range of styles and sub-genres.*

**Gilles Peterson (right)**
*Gilles Peterson has become famous for 'joining the dots' between dance music styles from around the world, including African and South American sounds.*

## MIXING IT UP

The more you understand about dance music and its history, the easier it is to see the connections between the different styles, and how they can be played together. Some styles can be easily mixed together using beat-matching techniques, while others can't. The best way to learn is simply to mix, trying different combinations of songs and styles. Some mixes will sound jarring, while others will be harmonious and complementary.

Joining the dots becomes easier if you vary your mixing style. Many DJs can get hung up on beat matching everything, but it is perfectly acceptable to change the tempo or vibe of a DJ set by simply dropping in a track when another has finished. Sometimes, this will get a far better response from dancers. Don't be afraid to try things; after all, there's nothing worse than a boring DJ who just plays it safe all the time.

# BUILDING & ORGANIZING YOUR MUSIC COLLECTION

As a DJ, the CDs, vinyl records or MP3 files you own are the tools of your trade. The best DJs not only build up a great collection of killer tracks, but also keep them neatly filed and organized.

Building a collection of music takes time. If you've been a committed music fan for some time, it is likely you already have a decent number of records, CDs or MP3 files. This is a great starting point, but you can never have too many options. Owning a sizeable music collection not only allows you to play different songs every time you DJ, but also makes mixing more enjoyable.

> **DJ TIP:** Some vinyl DJs like to have the BPM of a song to hand, in order to speed up the process of selecting and mixing records. They do this by noting down the tempo on a sticker, which they then place on the sleeve of the record.

**Digging**
*The art of sifting through second-hand records looking for gems is known in DJ circles as 'crate-digging'. The best crate-diggers are capable of sniffing out weird, wonderful and obscure records in odd places, often for incredibly cheap prices. For some, hunting for records in this way is almost as fun as DJing!*

**From A to Z**

*Many DJs file their records in a similar way to record shops, arranging them in alphabetical order by artist name. Others, though, prefer to cluster them together by style. As long as you can find what you're looking for quickly, you can organize your music however you want.*

## GET ORGANIZED

Whatever the size of your collection, it is important to keep it organized. If you don't, you will waste valuable time searching – time you could be spending mixing, or preparing for a gig.

There are many different ways to organize a music collection. Some DJs file their records and CDs by musical style, by tempo, or in A to Z order. This could be A to Z by artist name, or by record label.

Those who use MP3 files often store their music on portable hard drives, organizing them into folders by musical style or sub-genre. There is no set way to organize your music; the best way is whichever makes most sense to you.

## ON THE FLIPSIDE

Whichever way you organize your music, it is important to know your collection inside out. You may have bought something because you want to play a particular track, but is there a tasty remix or bonus track lurking elsewhere on the release? One day, that might be exactly the right song to set a dancefloor alight, change the mood, or take your mix to the next level. Unless you develop a deep knowledge of your collection, you'll never have these options.

**Flash Drives**

*Many digital DJs now store their music collection on portable flash drives, such as these USB sticks. Songs are often gathered together on different drives by style or artist.*

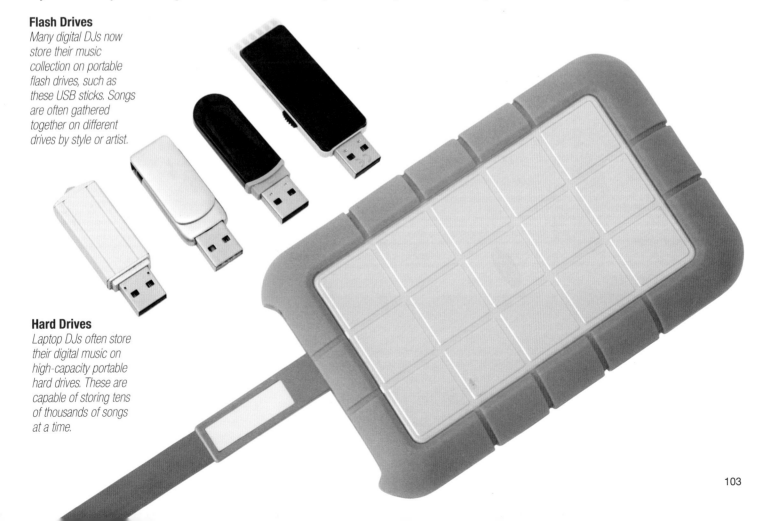

**Hard Drives**

*Laptop DJs often store their digital music on high-capacity portable hard drives. These are capable of storing tens of thousands of songs at a time.*

# ZANE LOWE

## 1973–

**RECOMMENDED LISTENING:**

*Breaks Co-Op – Roofers* (album, 1997)

*Kasabian – Vlad The Impaler* [Zane Lowe Remix] (single, 2008)

Zane Lowe is proof that DJs with wide-ranging music taste can prosper. During his time presenting shows on MTV and the UK's BBC Radio 1, he became renowned as a 'taste-maker', famous for playing the best indie-rock and dance music.

Born and raised in New Zealand, Lowe got involved with DJing and music production as a teenager. He was part of a band called Breaks Co-Op, who mixed up elements of breakbeat, hip-hop, jazz and downtempo beats. After the trio released their debut album *Roofers* in 1997, Lowe decided to move to the UK.

When he arrived in London, Lowe found a job working in a record shop. While there, he was spotted by radio station XFM. After successfully covering for another DJ, he was offered his own show.

It was when he moved to BBC Radio 1 in 2003 that Lowe's international reputation began to grow. He became known as someone who didn't shy away from playing music in a wide range of genres, championing both rock and electronic styles. Lowe cemented this reputation through DJ sets at clubs and festivals around the world.

Lowe finally left BBC Radio 1 in 2015, taking up a job presenting radio shows and compiling playlists for Apple Music's Beats 1 streaming service.

**Super Selector**

*Zane Lowe built his reputation not on technical mixing skills, but rather his ability to find and champion great music from a wide range of genres. It is for this reason that he is regarded as a taste-maker.*

FAVOURED STYLES:

**INDIE-ROCK
INDIE-DANCE
EDM**

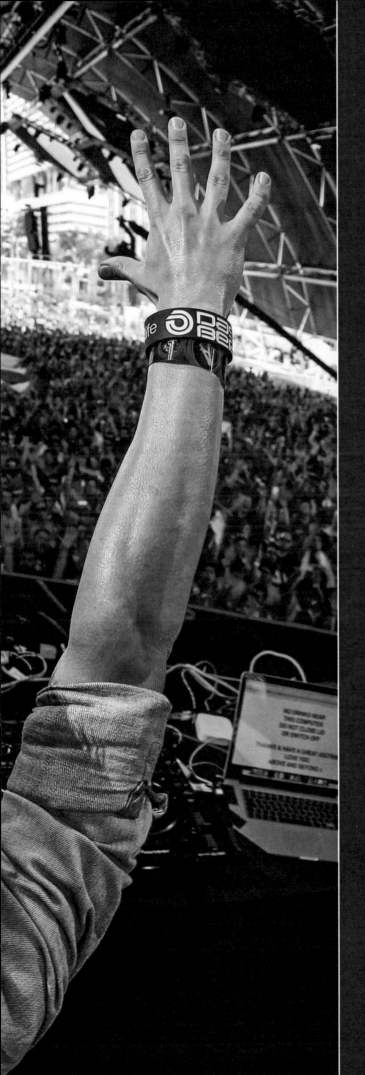

# CHAPTER 7:

# FROM PLAYING AT HOME TO PLAYING OUT

By now, you should be itching to showcase your newfound DJ skills on members of the public. It's time to graduate from the bedroom to the club...

**LEFT:** There's nothing quite like the buzz of playing in front of large crowds of people, especially when they respond enthusiastically to your selections and mixing.

# FROM NOVICE TO MAESTRO

There's more to being a great DJ than top tune selection and faultless mixing skills. You can work on these at home, but to become a true DJ hero you need practical experience of DJing in front of people.

**Pub DJ**
*Playing in pubs and bars isn't glamorous, but it does give up-and-coming DJs the chance to play long sets, showcase their skills in public, and learn how to respond to demanding punters.*

DJs are meant to be entertainers. Their job is to mix the music they love in order to get – or keep – people dancing. Do you have what it takes to do this, while taking the crowd on a musical journey?

The only way to find out is to play in front of people. It is a huge step for any DJ, and some never make it. Instead, they prefer to mix at home, DJing simply as a hobby. This is perfectly natural, although you're missing out on a huge part of the DJing experience if you never make it out of your living room.

## THE LEADER OF THE BAND

In some ways, the relationship between a DJ and their audience is similar to that of a band. Musicians are often inspired to deliver even better performances by enthusiastic and vocal crowds. DJs, too, feed off the

atmosphere and energy of their audiences, tailoring their sets to the reaction of dancers. If the crowd is going wild, the DJ will try to harness that energy for as long as possible. Alternatively, if there is no energy to feed off, then it is the DJ's job to create it.

## READY TO PARTY

In this chapter, we're going to discuss aspects of DJing specific to playing in front of people. The skills we'll discuss, such as understanding the reactions of dancers and building a DJ set, are what separate great DJs from also-rans. We're also going to talk about how to secure sets and how to prepare for that important first gig. By the end of the chapter, you'll be ready to rock club dancefloors.

**Practising at Home**
*There are few shortcuts to DJ success. The only way to sharpen your skills and learn the best ways to mix between songs in your collection is through hours of practice. Happily, this is an enjoyable way to spend your time!*

**Wedding Receptions (below)**
*Functions such as wedding receptions can be hard-going for beginners, but they do offer a good opportunity to develop your skills. People at these kinds of functions are normally in the mood to dance, and will respond positively if you play music they know.*

# SECURING YOUR FIRST DJ GIG

DJing is a competitive business, especially if you live in a big city. You can't expect that elusive first DJ booking to just fall into your lap. Instead, you need to actively seek out opportunities to showcase your skills.

Every DJ remembers the first time they played in front of people. It may have been during a house party, round a friend's flat, in a bar, or during a showcase of up-and-coming DJs at a local club. This first experience may or may not have gone well for them, but it may just have changed their life. For many people this will be the stepping stone they need to get started.

## START SMALL, THINK BIG

As a novice, you can't expect to be playing the best slots at the best clubs. You have to prove yourself, and that means starting at the bottom and working your way up. For now, you just need an opportunity of any kind, be it playing to friends, mixing background music in a bar, or supporting a higher-profile local or international DJ in a club.

**Who You Know**
*Sometimes, securing that elusive first gig can just be a matter of knowing the right people. Do any of your friends promote club events, run venues or book DJs for parties? If not, could they introduce you to people who do?*

## POSITIVE EDUCATION

Playing in front of friends is a good way to start, as they will naturally be supportive, and may have similar taste in music to you. Invite a few people round to your house for the evening, and try to keep them entertained by mixing up a great selection of music. If a friend is hosting a social event, offer to DJ at it – even if it means taking your own equipment along.

## HUNTING FOR GIGS

If you get a positive reaction from friends, try sniffing out other opportunities at recognized venues. Talk to bar managers, club owners and DJs at regular events you enjoy attending. If you play a particular type of music, seek out club nights that showcase these sounds, and offer your services to the promoters. Expect a few knock-backs, but sooner or later you'll get the chance you crave. If all else fails, you can always book a venue and put on your own party.

**House Party (below)**
*Playing to friends at a house party is a great way to start showcasing your skills in public. They may have similar tastes in music, and will naturally be more supportive than strangers.*

**Do It Yourself (right)**
*Many novice DJs book venues and put on their own club events. If you choose this route, you'll need to work hard at marketing, putting up posters and utilizing social media.*

# RECORDING YOUR FIRST DEMO MIX

Very few venue owners or club promoters will book a DJ without hearing them first. Because of this, most DJs record demo mixes at home to showcase their skills and help secure gigs.

A demo mix is exactly as it sounds: a demonstration recording of a DJ performance made for promotional purposes. Today, demo mixes are normally recorded as an MP3 (either on a portable digital recorder, or into a computer using a sound card or an audio interface), and either uploaded to the Internet (for example, onto sites such as Mixcloud, Hearthis and Soundcloud), or burned onto CD-Rs.

**Get Burning**
*If you're happy with your mix, don't hesitate to burn copies of it onto CD. These can then be handed to club contacts or posted through the mail. If you run out, just burn some more!*

**Inputs and Outputs**
*To record onto a portable recorder such as this, you'll need the correct leads to connect it to the back of your mixer. This model needs RCA phono to quarter-inch jack leads, but other recorders may have different connections.*

## DIG DEEP

Your demo mix is a chance to show off a little. Musically, there are no rules, though the mix should feature the genre, or genres, you wish to play in bars or clubs. Over the course of an hour, it should take the listener on a journey, and contain a mixture of well-known tracks, lesser-known remixes and surprising selections. Anyone can mix together 10 or 15 currently popular tracks; not everyone can contrast these with forgotten older records or obscure underground selections.

## GET MIXING

Before recording your demo mix, spend some time playing around at home, trying out different mixes and combinations of tracks. When you think you have come up with the perfect running order, do a number of practice runs to get each of the mixes as tight as they can be. Once you're happy, record the mix. Remember: if you make mistakes or aren't happy with how something sounds, you can always start again.

**Keeping Track**

*When putting together their first demo mix, many DJs find it useful to make a track list, with additional notes about specific blends. This can include details of when to mix the tracks together, as well as the projected running order.*

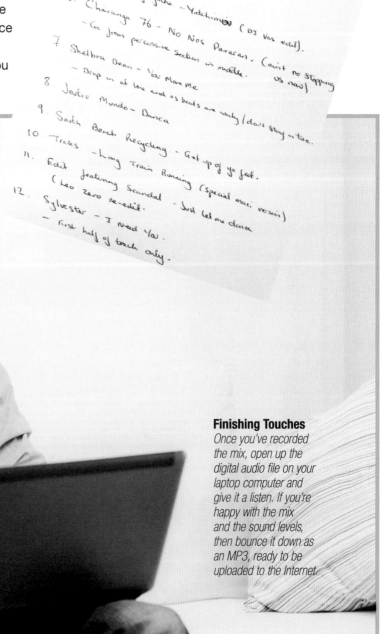

**Finishing Touches**

*Once you've recorded the mix, open up the digital audio file on your laptop computer and give it a listen. If you're happy with the mix and the sound levels, then bounce it down as an MP3, ready to be uploaded to the Internet.*

# PREPARING FOR YOUR FIRST DJ GIG

Having secured that elusive first DJ gig, make sure you take some time to get fully prepared. You'll need to select tracks, and pack a box or bag with all the music and equipment you will need.

The first thing to consider is where and when you'll be playing. Unless the venue owner has given you clear instructions, you'll need to use your judgment as to what music will be appropriate. If you've been given an early warm-up slot, then you'll be expected to set the tone and gently tease people onto the dancefloor. If you're on later – what DJs refer to as peak time – then dancers may be expecting heavier music.

## PICKING TRACKS

Select tracks that you know go well together, and that you are comfortable mixing. It's fine to have a specific set or sequence of tracks in mind, but you need to be prepared to change tack if necessary. Pack more music than you'll have a chance to play, including a few better-known tracks to drop if people aren't responding to your chosen set.

**Selections**
*Take your time over selecting music to take with you. Allow a few hours to select and pack records, CDs or digital playlists.*

**Double-check**
*Some DJs find it useful to gather together and lay out everything they'll need before packing their bag. Here are the typical contents of a DVS DJ's gig bag, including timecode vinyl, audio interface, headphones, leads, laptop and spare needles.*

**Box Fresh**
*When packing your record box or bag, think about how to arrange the music within it. The records could be ordered by BPM (with the slowest at the front of the bag, and the fastest at the back), in the sequence in which you wish to play them, or clustered together by style.*

**Timecode control vinyl**

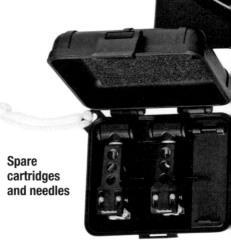

**Spare cartridges and needles**

### BPM Guides

*Some DJs like to note down the tempo of their records, in beats per minute, somewhere on their records (or, to protect the artwork, on stickers placed on protective plastic sleeves). This is particularly good for beginners, who don't have the level of experience to quickly calculate the BPM of a track while DJing.*

A1 - 118 BPM
A2 - 108 BPM
B - 109 BPM

### OTHER ESSENTIALS

Your box or bag should also contain any equipment you will need to perform, such as:

• Headphones.
• Spare slipmats, cartridges and needles (vinyl or DVS DJs).
• Laptop and mains lead.
• DVS audio interface, timecode control discs, audio and USB leads.
• DJ or MIDI controller with USB and audio leads.

Headphones

Laptop

Hard drive

VINYL VAULT
ANOTHER DR.SUZUKI PRODUCTION
MADE IN JAPAN

Audio interface box

RANE SL2
serato

Phono leads

USB leads

# THE DYNAMICS OF A DJ SET

There is no 'correct' way to perform a DJ set, but there are a few things to bear in mind before you set out for the club. These tips and tricks will help to keep you on the right track.

**Empty Club**
*Many inexperienced DJs are offered warm-up slots, which are traditionally in the first two hours after a club opens. Warming up is a useful skill to learn, as even some experienced DJs find it hard to do.*

**Busy Club (right)**
*If you're lucky enough to play to a packed dancefloor, grasp the opportunity with both hands. If people are already having a good time, your job is simply to keep them happy. Sometimes, that's easy; at other times, it can be quite demanding.*

## KNOW YOUR ROLE

Where will your DJ set feature in the night? Finding this out will give you a clearer idea what sort of set you should play.

### • The warm-up

This is the early slot, traditionally when clubs are quieter. The warm-up DJ's job is to create a good atmosphere, to gently tease people onto the dancefloor, and to conserve energy levels. You should resist the temptation to go too fast, too soon.

### • Peak time

These are the slots that novice DJs dream of playing. Peak-time DJs are expected to make sure dancers have the time of their lives. You can play as big, bold, fast and tough as you like, but be careful not to tire out dancers too quickly.

### • End of night

Closing the party can be an honour or a chore, depending on how many people have stayed. Send people home happy by playing a mix of club classics and surprising selections.

## THINK ABOUT STRUCTURE

Before you head to the gig, work out how you would like to start and end your set, then fill in the gap. If you plan to finish with a track that is significantly faster than the one you started with, the songs in between should subtly increase in tempo.

## HANDLE WITH CARE

Try to grab people's attention by starting with a memorable or well-known track. After that, try to avoid playing too many obvious songs. Crowds soon come to expect big tunes if that's all you play, so it's best to ration them.

## BE FLEXIBLE

Each DJ set should be an expression of your musical taste and DJ style, adjusted to suit the demands of the venue and its clientele. Don't be afraid to adapt your approach in order to make the set a success.

# IN THE CLUB

Performing in a venue is very different to playing a DJ set at home. Knowing what to expect when you arrive will help cut down on unnecessary stress and worry, while easing the inevitable first-night nerves.

Try to arrive at the venue with plenty of time to spare. This will allow you to assess your surroundings, take a look at the DJ booth – if there is one – and the way the equipment is set up. If another DJ is playing, take time to listen to the tracks they're playing, while watching the response of dancers. You may need to adjust your plans by selecting a different starting tune, or playing a slightly different set.

> **DJ TIP:** When you begin, it may take a little time to adjust to the feel of the equipment you are playing on. This is only to be expected. Your confidence will grow once you've nailed a few mixes, so concentrate hard and keep it simple – you can always bring out the tricks and trademark blends later in the set.

**Don't Stress!**
*If things go wrong, or the club's set-up is confusing, don't get stressed. Take a few deep breaths, and try to calmly work out what you can do to address the situation.*

**Rotary Mixers**
*Some venues, particularly those in the United States, feature mixers without faders. These are known as rotary mixers, because the controls are all based on rotary knobs. If you come across one of these, take extra time to work out the controls before you start.*

## INSIDE THE DJ BOOTH

It's likely that the club's equipment will be very different to what you are used to mixing on. Have a long look at the mixer to make sure you know where all the key controls are, and which channels each sound source is plugged in to. Is there a monitor speaker to help you mix? If so, where is it, and how do you adjust the volume?

### Expect the Unexpected

*Every DJ booth differs, and occasionally you'll come across equipment you've not used, or even seen, before. This DJ booth features vintage Pioneer CDJ-1000 turntables, which are much more basic than contemporary CD turntables.*

If you're planning to use any of your own equipment, such as a laptop and DVS audio interface, make sure that it's all set up and working before your allotted set time.

# LEARNING FROM EXPERIENCE

The best DJs seem to instinctively know exactly what to play, and when. This is partly due to experience and musical knowledge, but also their ability to read a dancefloor. If you want to be a great DJ, this is a skill you need to learn.

Being able to read a dancefloor is a skill that all great DJs possess. If you want to give it a try, simply watch the body language of club-goers and dancers during your sets. Pay close attention to how they react to each record, and particular musical traits.

- How are they dancing? Are they really going for it, or are they merely shuffling?
- Do they look like they have bags of energy, or are they flagging a little?
- Do they seem to prefer a particular sub-genre, such as

**Bored Crowd**

*These club-goers look a little bored, as if they are waiting to be entertained or inspired. Try surprising them by dramatically altering the style of music you're playing, or dropping an older, well-known record they might not have heard in years.*

acid house or deep house, or are they keener to hear a wider range of sounds?

- Do they maintain interest during long tracks, or does their attention wane?
- Are they happy to dance to music they don't know, or do they only respond to tracks they know?
- Do they respond more enthusiastically to songs with certain characteristics, such as funky basslines, prominent vocals or heavier drumbeats?
- Are they really into it, or do they look like they need to hear something that will inspire them?

## SEVENTH SENSE

This may seem a little complex, but with more experience of playing out it will soon become second nature. You will instinctively know when to change tack, alter your mixing style, throw more energetic records into the mix, and drop big tunes. You won't always get it right, but with every misjudgment you will learn something new.

**Going Crazy**
*If you're getting this reaction, things are going pretty well! Your next task is to harness this enthusiasm and the dancers' energy level to keep the party going for longer. That might seem easy, but sometimes it's even harder than inspiring a bored crowd.*

# ANDY C

## 1976–

RECOMMENDED LISTENING:
*Ram Raiders* – The Mix (DJ mix, 2001)
*Nightlife 6* (DJ mix, 2013)

Few would argue with the notion that Andy C is the greatest drum & bass DJ ever. In fact, in a 2014 poll of fellow international DJs, he was voted the fourth best DJ of all time.

Andy C initially made his name as a music producer and record label owner. Alongside friend Ant Miles, he established jungle imprint Ram Records in 1992. A year later, the pair teamed up in the studio as Origin Unknown, unleashing the track 'Valley Of The Shadows'. It's now considered one of the greatest drum & bass records of all time.

From the start, Andy C was regarded as one of jungle and drum & bass's most technically gifted, adventurous and entertaining DJs. Utilizing turntablism skills more often associated with hip-hop, he rattles through tracks at a furious rate, often using three Technics turntables. He has also developed his own signature mix, known as the 'double drop', using two copies of the same record to introduce the bassline at the same time.

This trademark DJ style, coupled with a love of representing all forms of jungle and drum & bass, has made Andy C one of the most popular DJs on the planet. To date, he has won the People's Award for Best DJ at the Drum & Bass Arena Awards every year since its inception in 2009.

**Rare Success**
*Although he has produced some superb records over the years, Andy C's success is primarily down to his top-drawer DJ skills. This makes him a rarity in today's dance music scene, as the majority of big-name DJs owe their fame to successful production careers.*

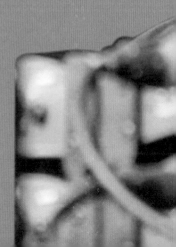

FAVOURED STYLES:

**JUNGLE
DRUM & BASS**

# THE
# FUTURE

Now you've mastered mixing and delivered your first performances, it's time to focus on building up your DJ career.

LEFT: Many DJs boost their careers by also becoming music producers. Making dance music is not easy, but having a DJ's understanding of what works on dancefloors is a great foundation for future production success.

# DEVELOPING YOUR DJ STYLE

As you get more experience of DJing in front of people, you'll begin to learn which combinations of tracks get the best reaction. Naturally, you'll begin to develop a more distinctive DJ style that more accurately reflects your taste in music.

**Dam Funk**
*Los Angeles-based musician, producer and DJ Dam Funk is known for performing sets that blur the boundaries between DJing and live performance. He frequently interrupts DJ sets to perform his own songs using a 'keytar', a 1980s keyboard that is worn around the neck like a guitar.*

All the greatest DJs, past and present, have their own trademark styles, developed through years of collecting music and mixing tracks. Some, such as DJ Harvey, Laurent Garnier and Danny Tenaglia, are renowned for taking dancers on a journey over five or six hours. Others, such as drum & bass legend DJ Marky, are famous for including amazing turntable tricks as part of their performance.

## GET CREATIVE

Finding your style can come through experimentation as much as experience. Don't be afraid to try things out at home, to see what they sound like. By combining elements of different musical styles, you may accidentally create something really special.

That's what happened in the mid-1990s, when a group of London DJs began speeding up US garage records, and

**Record Your Own Sounds**
*With a microphone and a portable recorder, you could record your own sound effects to add extra textures and noises to your DJ set. Many portable recorders have good-quality microphones built in, or you can buy a separate microphone to plug in.*

**Danny Tenaglia (right)**
*Since first emerging at the start of the 1990s, Danny Tenaglia has become famous for playing marathon DJ sets that can last for 10 or 12 hours at a time. He uses this time to take dancers on a journey using long mixes between songs, and even longer tracks.*

combining them with the weighty basslines of drum & bass. It wasn't long before producers began making records in this style, which became known as UK garage.

## FIND YOUR TRUE CALLING

You don't have to be that innovative to stand out from the crowd, but you do have to find your own niche. Whether it's energetically mashing up loads of tracks quickly, jumping between different musical styles or simply playing one sub-genre better than anyone else, you stand more chance of success if you are unique.

**Expand Your Horizons**
*When visiting record shops, don't be afraid to listen to music in styles other than the ones you're most comfortable playing. You might find something that can take your DJing in a different direction, or will help lift your sets to a whole new level.*

127

# MASHING IT UP

It may take some time to develop a distinctive DJ style, but there are things you can try now that will make your sets come alive. We're talking about making use of all the tools at your disposal, regardless of whether you are a vinyl, CD or laptop DJ.

## SPECIAL EFFECTS

If you mix using DJ software, you may already have used some of the creative functions in your sets, such as loops, sample banks and special effects. Many mixers installed in clubs also boast effects features, allowing you to alter the sound of your sets by adding echo, phasing, filters and other cool sounds.

## LIVE LOOPING

Live looping involves taking a short section of a track and repeating it, either to tease out a groove in order to build tension, or to make longer mixes possible. Many CD turntables boast this feature, while vinyl DJs can achieve the same effect by mixing between two copies of the same record.

**A-Trak**
*Since starting out as a hip-hop DJ, A-Trak has developed his style. Now, he's best known for playing sets where he quickly mashes up beats, vocals and samples from many different songs and sound sources.*

**Mash-up Singles (above)**
*It's not uncommon to come across mash-up records, which blend elements of two or more well-known songs to create something new and, crucially, dancefloor-friendly.*

**Reel to Reel (below)**
*In the 1970s and 1980s, some DJs took reel-to-reel tape machines to the club with them. They would use them to add sound effects, or play their own unique, homemade re-edits of songs.*

**Bootleg Remixes (above)**
*Promotional copies of singles by big R&B, hip-hop and pop artists, including Beyoncé, often feature acapella recordings of their vocals. Record labels do this to encourage DJs to use them creatively, and even make their own bootleg remixes.*

## USING ACAPELLA TRACKS

These are vocal tracks without any musical accompaniment. They can often be found lurking on the B-sides of old house, disco, hip-hop and R&B records. Playing a familiar vocal from a classic song over the top of a brand new instrumental track is a classic DJ trick.

## MIXING WITH DJ TOOLS & BATTLE BREAKS

Some dance music releases include DJ tools or beats versions of the main song. These are extended drum tracks, designed for use in DJ sets. They can be layered over other tracks, used as a bridge between songs, or be combined with acapella tracks to create unique new songs.

## VERSIONING

Many dance singles feature multiple versions, or remixes, of the same song. Why not create your own version by blending bits of several remixes during your performance?

# BUILDING YOUR PROFILE

Competition between DJs for bookings can be fierce. You will stand a better chance of getting club sets if you build up a fan base. In this day and age, the easiest way to do that is using online promotion.

Venue owners and club promoters may be music lovers, but first and foremost they are business people. One of the factors they often look at before booking a DJ is how popular they are. In other words, will the DJ's appearance get more people through doors?

One of the things they consider is the DJ's online presence. Does he or she have profile pages on social media networks such as Facebook and Twitter? If so, how many 'likes' and 'followers' do they have?

**DJ TIP:** Another great way of promoting yourself is to start your own blog or website. This could contain news, details of forthcoming appearances, your thoughts on new music releases, links to interesting online articles, and regular DJ mixes or radio show recordings.

## STREAMING SERVICES

As well as social media profiles, many DJs also have their own pages on music streaming sites such as Mixcloud and Soundcloud. These are used to host demo mixes and recordings of their DJ performances. In many ways, these kinds of profiles are more important than social media networks, as potential fans can hear you in action. Regular mixes mean regular listeners, and subsequently more potential customers for the venues you play at.

## RADIO GAGA

Another great way of reaching a new audience is to host your own radio show. This can be used to showcase your DJ skills, and the quality of your music collection. Local community stations are often looking for volunteers to host shows, while there are a large number of specialist Internet radio stations aimed at underground dance music lovers. These will often award shows to little-known DJs if they have a good idea and a blinding record collection.

### Listening on the Go
*Portable Internet access, smartphones and streaming services have changed the way people listen to music. Add your DJ mixes to streaming services and people can listen to you worldwide.*

### Going Live
*It can be hard to secure shows on professional radio stations, but online dance stations are always looking for DJs. You can usually produce, present and mix these shows from your home.*

# THE IMPORTANCE OF PRODUCTION

Music production is another great way to raise your profile and enhance your DJ sets. Many of today's most high-profile DJs are also highly regarded music producers – some even began their careers as musicians, before turning their hand to DJing.

## THE ROAD TO SUCCESS

Eats Everything is one of underground house music's most popular DJs, who regularly plays to thousands of people at massive club events and music festivals. He gets well rewarded for his endeavours, and is regularly paid large sums of money for appearances.

Yet it wasn't so long ago that he was plain old Dan Pearce, a jobbing DJ in his home city of Bristol. He was well known on the city's club scene, but could hardly have been considered a big player. Then, in 2011, he released his first music productions under the Eats Everything name. A year later, he was one of the most in-demand DJs in the UK.

**Deetron**
*Techno and house DJ Samuel Geiser, better known as Deetron, is arguably more famous for his music productions. These productions keep his profile high, making it more likely that he'll be booked to play DJ sets.*

**Inspiration**
*Ideas for music productions can strike at any moment, even during DJ sets. For example, combining DJ tools such as drum tracks and acapellas could offer a rough template for a mash-up remix.*

**Headhunterz (below)**
*Although a DJ from an early age, hardstyle and EDM star Headhunterz owes much of his success to a prolific production career that stretches back to the mid-2000s. He has released many singles, plus countless remixes and DJ mix CDs.*

## WHY PRODUCTION MATTERS

Dan Pearce's story is remarkable, but it's not uncommon for DJs' careers to blossom on the back of successful music productions. If you create a track that becomes a club anthem – even in underground clubs – then you will quickly become an in-demand DJ. Of course, few people will be quite as successful as Pearce has been.

Even so, it's worth considering turning your hand to production. Later in this chapter, we'll outline different methods of creating unique pieces of music. Whether these are signed by record labels or not, they can be used to add a level of exclusivity to your DJ sets. If people want to hear your productions – to begin with, at least – then they'll have to attend your club appearances.

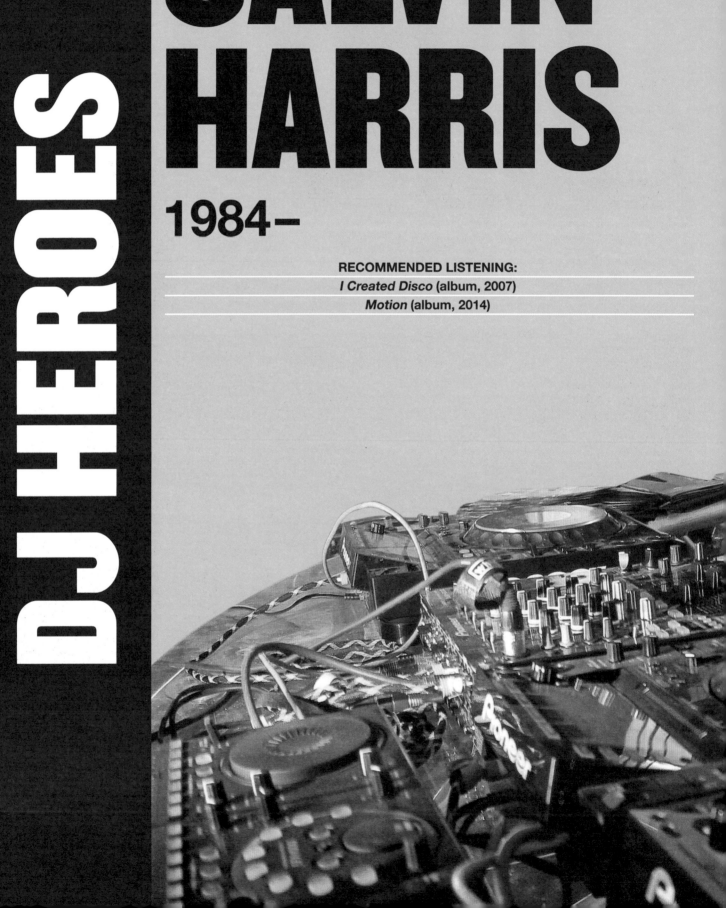

# DJ HEROES

# CALVIN HARRIS

## 1984–

RECOMMENDED LISTENING:
*I Created Disco* (album, 2007)
*Motion* (album, 2014)

**Earning Power**
*Only a fraction of Calvin Harris' colossal earnings come from DJ fees. Having written and produced some of the most popular dance songs, he earns royalty payments each time one is played on the radio, television or the Internet. He can also command large payments to produce records for other people, such as pop star Rihanna.*

FAVOURED
STYLES:

# DANCE-POP
# ELECTRO HOUSE
# EDM

# CREDIT TO THE EDIT

Many DJs enter music production by creating their own re-edits of songs. These are rearrangements of existing tracks that have been altered to either make them more DJ-friendly, or more appropriate for their DJ sets.

DJs have been making their own rearrangements of tracks since the 1970s. During the disco era, popular DJs, such as Larry Levan, Danny Krivit and François Kevorkian, would re-edit tracks by cutting and splicing together reel-to-reel tapes. By taking a tape machine with them to clubs, they could wow crowds with these one-off versions.

## COMPUTER EDITING

Re-editing is a much easier process today. All you need is some free audio-editing software, such as Audacity, a laptop computer, and a bunch of tracks to rearrange. Using the software, you can easily extend passages of the tracks you like, emphasize certain elements, or remove bits of the song altogether. Once you learn how to use the software, you can prepare edits of tracks quickly, export them as an MP3 file, and then test them out in your DJ sets.

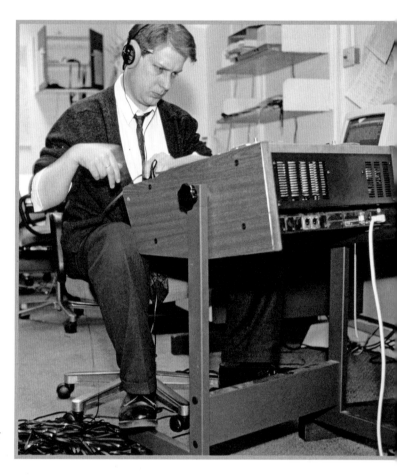

**The Edit Screen**
*This is what a song looks like when it's loaded into Audacity. The beginning of the track features four repetitions, the latter of which merges into the rest of the song. All the tools you'll need to edit the song can be found in the toolbar at the top of the edit screen.*

**Razor and Tape (right)**
*Re-editing music used to be a long process. It involved manually slicing, rearranging and sticking together lengths of quarter-inch magnetic tape. Early DJ re-editors were therefore made to work hard when creating their own bespoke versions of songs.*

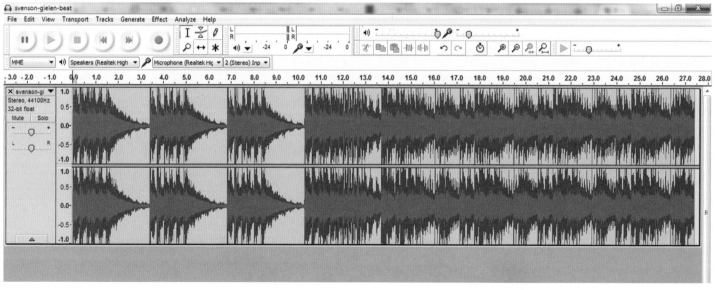

**Danny Krivit (above)**
*Disco and house DJ Danny Krivit is widely regarded as one of the world's best re-editors. The New Yorker made his first re-edits in the late 1970s using reel-to-reel tape machines.*

**Dancefloor-driven (right)**
*The best re-edits will always get a better reaction from dancers than the original versions. This is because they are created with clubs in mind, rather than for the radio or home listening.*

## DANCEFLOOR REARRANGEMENTS

So what makes a good re-edit? It's a difficult question to answer. Many of the best re-edits either lengthen short tracks to make them more suitable for club use, extend drum patterns to make mixing easier, or remove sections of the song that are dubious, unnecessary or plain rubbish. Some re-edits breathe new life into forgotten or little-known songs, while others make a popular track more 'playable'. All re-edits have one thing in common: they make the track being rearranged more dancefloor-friendly.

# COPYRIGHT

**Many DJs have enjoyed a career boost after sharing their re-edits on the Internet, or releasing them as white label vinyl records. Although this is illegal unless you own the copyright to the original track (this is usually held by the record label who first released it), this hasn't stopped DJs doing it.**

# REMIX CULTURE

As long as there has been dance music, DJs have made their own remixes and mash-ups. There's a long history, too, of these remixes becoming club hits, offering a much-needed boost to DJs' careers.

The hip-hop DJ/producer Danger Mouse owes his fame, in part at least, to *The Grey Album*, an illegal CD he produced containing unique remixes of tracks from Jay-Z's *Black Album*. He combined Jay-Z's vocals with new tracks he'd made out of short samples of The Beatles' *White Album*. The record was leaked on the Internet and downloaded many hundreds of thousands of times, making Danger Mouse a star.

## REMIX, RE-FIX

A remix differs from a re-edit in that it can be more than a simple rearrangement of a song. It usually contains a mixture of elements from the song being reworked, plus new sounds, drumbeats and samples added by the DJ or producer.

### 2 Many DJs (above)
*Belgian DJ/production duo 2 Many DJs rose to fame in the early 2000s with a series of mix CDs that saw them join the dots between a number of different musical styles. They did this by sampling and mashing together elements of lots of different records.*

### Akai S1000 (below)
*The explosion in dance music remix culture can be traced back to the Akai S1000, a classic and cutting-edge piece of production hardware. It allowed producers to record, or 'sample', short sections of music, then manipulate them in different ways.*

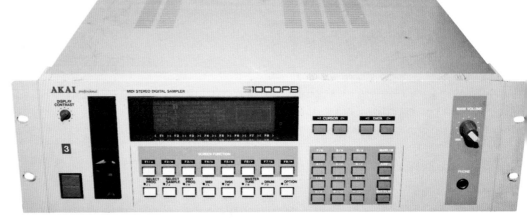

**Illegal Gains (left)**
*What Danger Mouse did with the music of The Beatles and Jay-Z was hugely creative, but also illegal. Although the remaining members of The Beatles and Jay-Z both liked the results, it didn't stop their record labels threatening to sue Danger Mouse.*

**Beats & Pieces (above)**
*British dance music veterans Coldcut first found fame by creating a series of mash-up records based on samples of other people's music. They were then asked to remix a classic track by hip-hop act Eric B & Rakim in a similar style.*

Some remixes are officially produced and sanctioned, with record labels providing DJs with the constituent parts of the song (bassline, guitars, drums, vocals and so on). Other remixes are produced by DJs simply by taking (known as 'sampling') parts of somebody else's song and adding them to their own music.

## MASH IT UP

The simplest form of a remix is a 'mash-up'. This is when a DJ or producer combines two different songs to create a new one. Most 'mash-ups' simply place a vocal from one record over an instrumental version of another. A good example is The Source featuring Candi Staton's 'You Got The Love', which is now considered a house classic. It blends the vocal from Staton's 1986 song 'You Got The Love' with music based on Frankie Knuckles' 1987 house hit 'Your Love' (itself a remix of a track by Jamie Principle).

# PRODUCING ORIGINAL MUSIC

Making your own electronic music is time-consuming and can be a complex task for beginners. However, it is a step that many DJs take, and not just as a career move. If you are passionate about music, it is often the logical next step.

Thanks to a mix of user-friendly production software, cheaper equipment and beginner-friendly 'sample packs', making electronic music is easier now than it's ever been. Even so, taking up music production is not a step you should take lightly. Many DJs struggle to find enough time to practise mixing, develop their own style, record demo mixes and promote their careers, let alone learn how to make tracks.

## THE MUSIC-MAKING BUG

Music making is still something worth considering, though. Making music is a hugely creative and enjoyable hobby, and there is little else like the buzz of seeing a dancefloor going crazy to something that you have made. There is not space here to go into detail about how to produce music, but we can outline some of the software and equipment you will need.

**Simple set-up**
*Although it can still be expensive, putting together a simple home studio set-up is not that complicated. This one, featuring a blend of traditional instruments, electronic gear and a computer, is an excellent example of a basic but effective studio.*

## THE BEDROOM STUDIO

### Laptop/desktop computer & music production software

You will need a digital audio workstation (DAW). This is an all-in-one program that allows you to compose, record, arrange, produce and mix songs from scratch. Popular DAW software packages include Ableton Live, Logic Pro Audio, Pro Tools and Cubase.

### Sound card/audio interface

An essential purchase, this acts as an interface between music production equipment and your computer.

### MIDI keyboard

This can be used to play in (and record) musical elements. Some MIDI keyboards also contain other features to control aspects of the DAW software (effectively making them MIDI controllers).

### MIDI controller

For tapping in drum rhythms and controlling some functions of the DAW software.

### Monitor speakers

Use these to listen to the music you are making. Monitor

speakers can also be used with your DJ set-up, to make monitoring mixes easier.

### Mixing desk

This should be considered an optional extra, as you can prepare mix-downs of songs in most DAW software packages. A mixing desk becomes more essential if your production set-up contains hardware such as drum machines and synthesizers.

# GLOSSARY

**Ambient**
A style of instrumental music with electronic textures and no persistent beat, used to create or enhance a mood or atmosphere.

**Audio Interface**
Also known as a 'sound card', this device acts as an intermediary between a computer and sound sources. The black box at the heart of any Digital Vinyl System is an audio interface.

**Beat**
The pattern of drum sounds used to create a rhythm. If you nod your head to music you are nodding to the beat. If you count 4 nods at a time (1,2,3,4) you are counting 4 beats to a 'bar'.

**Beat match**
The process of setting the 'tempo/speed/pitch' of two songs so that they are playing at the same speed and time, in order to mix them together. When two songs are played together this way, DJs say they are 'beat matched'. Beat matching is a fundamental part of DJing.

**BPM**
Stands for Beats Per Minute. If you nod your head or tap your foot to music you are following the 'beat'. If you count how many nods or taps you do in a minute you have calculated the BPM.

**Channel**
An individual path way on a DJ mixer that music is played through. Each 'channel' has its own sound inputs, upfader, and EQ controls.

**CD (Compact Disc)**
A format of disc that contains music.

**CDJs**
DJ slang for CD turntables. These are CD players designed for use by DJs, and feature functions to help mixing (E.G song speed control).

**Copyright**
The legal proof that someone wrote the song you are using and that you should not copy, lend or borrow bits of their work without asking and/or paying them first.

**Controller**
'DJ Controllers' are hardware units containing all the functions a DJ would need in order to perform a set. The 'controller' unit connects to a PC or Mac computer running a DJ software program.

**Crossfader**
A control feature of DJ mixers that allows you to control which sound source (turntable one or two, for example) the audience hears.

**Cue**
To prepare a song to be played.

**Cut**
To quickly jump from one song to another using the mixer's crossfader.

**Deck**
DJ slang for a piece of equipment that plays CDs or vinyl records. More accurately referred to as a 'turntable'.

**Digital Vinyl System**
Also known as DVS, a digital vinyl system allows DJs to control music stored on their computer using traditional DJ equipment, such as CD or vinyl 'decks'. It does this using a special audio interface, which sits between the 'decks' and the computer, and specially designed DJ software.

**DJ Controller**
See 'controller'.

**DJ Mixer**
A DJ mixer allows you to play music from a number of different sound sources (for example CD or vinyl decks) and seamlessly transition between them.

**DJ Software**
Working with 'Digital Vinyl Systems' or 'DJ controllers', DJ Software uses the processors on Computers to play and manipulate sounds. Some DJ Software is intended to act alone without any 'CD' or 'Vinyl' players at all.

'**EDIT**' is generally used to mean the activity of altering any audio or video. In DJ circles, an 'edit' (or 're-edit') is also a special version of a song.

**EQ** – controls that let you affect different frequencies of sound on your songs. On DJ mixers these are normally 'HI/High/Treble/Top', 'Mid' and 'Bass/Low'.

**Fade**
Turn volume up or down so song begins or ends smoothly.

**Fader**
The fader is the controller we use to 'fade' a song. It can either increase or decrease volume smoothly.

**Filter**
A type of FX.

**FX [Effects]**
Controls that let you do all kinds of things to the sound of your songs.

**Gain**
A control that can be used to boost, or cut, volume levels. This is different to the fader as it has much more power and is normally set using headphones and warning lights before you play any sound through your speakers.

**Headphone Monitor**
A control on a DJ mixer that allows you to monitor the sound levels of an individual channel on their mixer, the mixer's output, or a combination of the two. It is used by DJs before, and during mixes.

**Headphone Selector**
A control on a DJ mixer for choosing which channels sound is heard from in the headphones. It is usually used in conjunction with the 'headphone monitor'.

**Intro**
The beginning bit of a tune before all the instruments, riff or hook have really started.

**Jog Wheel**
A major feature of CD 'decks' and DJ controllers, the jog wheel is mainly used to subtly adjust the speed of a song during mixing.

**Loop**
Any bit of a song that you repeat. CD decks have buttons that let you set any part of the song (usually between 2 and 32 beats long) to loop. A good loop can become the basic beat or riff of a whole new song.

**MIDI controller**
So-called because it works on MIDI (short for Musical Instrument Digital Interface), this is a piece of equipment that can be set-up to control certain features of DJ, or music production software.

**Mix**
Any way you choose to swap between two songs during a DJ performance. A recording of a DJ's performance is also called a 'mix', or 'DJ mix'.

**Mixer**
See 'DJ mixer', above.

**Monitor Speaker**
A musical speaker designed and set-up to be used by a DJ during his or her performance. The 'monitor speaker' helps the DJ to keep track of what they're doing before, during, and after a mix.

**MP3**
A format for storing and playing music on computers, and other mobile electronic devices. MP3 files are popular due to their small file size, especially when compared to higher quality digital sound formats such as 'WAV' and 'AIFF'. Low-quality MP3s sound poor on large sound systems so you should use ones with a higher bit-rate and larger file size (ideally 320 kbps, which is the highest quality available).

**Outro**
The end of a song, often the same few words being faded out, or a the same few bars of music on repeat.

**'Original mix'**
This is the original version of a song as composed and produced by the artist.

**Phono**
Phono level relates only to vinyl decks – be sure to put the cable from any vinyl turntable into a phono input on your DJ mixer. Any digital equipment, such as CD decks, should be plugged into the 'line' inputs on your mixer.

**Phono Cable**
Also called RCA, the industry standard cable for DJ and home hifi equipment.

**Pitch**
Sometimes confused with speed or tempo, the pitch of music is actually the frequency of the waveform, which enables us to hear music. The pitch of a sound defines it's note.

**Platter**
In the case of vinyl decks, the platter is the portion of the turntable that spins, and on which the record sits during playback.

**Pitch Control Fader**
The control used to alter the speed or tempo of music on DJ equipment. See also 'Pitch'.

**Pulse**
Same as 'beat.'

**'REMIX'**
This is a version of a song that uses some of the original parts of the song but may have other musical elements to it. 'Remixes' can be done by the original artist, or by other artists.

**'Re-master'**
Normally used to describe an old song that has been re-processed by a music producer or sound engineer, in order to make it sound better on modern sound reproduction equipment.

**Riff**
The recognizable bit of a song you remember, hum, or sing along to.

**RPM**
Short for 'revolutions per minute', RPM refers to the number of times a turntable's platter goes round in a minute. Most turntables have two settings (33rpm and 45rpm). Make sure you check the labels of your vinyl records to find out which of these settings you should use to play it.

**Sample**
Any bit of music used to make new music, often a drum break, stab, or short section of a vocal (e.g. a sentence from a rap track, or a few words of singing).

**Scratch**
A sound created by moving a vinyl record, or the jog wheel of a CD turntable, back and forth. There are a number of different 'scratches' that can be performed by DJs.

**Scribbling**
A basic scratch technique where you just move back and forward quickly around a sound – experiment, you may find you like it!

**Slip-cueing**
The process of holding a vinyl record in place while the platter spins below, before releasing it at the right moment. Once 'released', the record will play as normal.

**Slipmat**
A round piece of felt, or cloth, that sits on the platter of a vinyl turntable. It allows the DJ to hold or manipulate a vinyl record, while the platter keeps spinning below.

**Software**
A computer application, sometimes known as a 'program', designed to fulfill a specific task (e.g. help you perform a DJ set, send emails, browse the Internet etc.)

**Soundcard**
See 'Audio Interface'.

**Sound System** – The amplifiers, speakers, outboard units and crossovers that together create the sound in clubs and venues. Not in anyway like a home HiFi or a portable P.A. The Sound System requires a 'Sound Engineer' to correctly use it.

**Speed** – also called tempo or sometimes pitch. This is the speed a song is playing at, and is measured in Beats Per Minute (BPM).

**Spindle**
The metal rod found poking through the centre of the platter on every vinyl turntable. It is designed to keep the vinyl record in place during play back.

**Split Cueing**
The 'split cue' feature found on some DJ mixers allows you to 'split' sounds between each of the headphone cups. For example, you could listen to the song you're about to mix in on the left side, and the track that's already playing on the right side.

**Stylus**
A diamond needle that's inserted into a cartridge fixed to the tone arm of a vinyl turntable. The stylus picks up vibrations from a vinyl record, turning them into the sounds we hear through the speakers.

**Tempo**
This is the speed a song is playing in, measured in Beats Per Minute (BPM).

**Timecode control discs**
Specially made vinyl records or CDs, which are used with Digital Vinyl Systems (DVS). They allow DJs to mix as they would with regular records or CDs, but contain a special 'timecode', rather than actual music, that sends instructions to DJ software loaded onto a laptop computer.

**Transformer**
A 'scratch' technique that uses the cross-fader to turn a sound 'on' and 'off', while another plays continuously.

**Turntable**
A 'deck.'

**Turntablism**
Using records or CDs to make your own music by scratching, juggling, sampling etc. instead of just playing the songs.

**Upfader**
The sound control fader found on each 'channel' on a DJ mixer. You push it up to turn up the volume.

**USB**
Short for 'Universal Serial Bus', USB is a type of computer connection. It can be used to connect different types of equipment (DJ controller, MIDI controller, smartphone, printer etc) to a laptop or desktop computer.

**Verse**
The bit of a song where the singer/ rapper sings the main part of the song.

**Vinyl**
A 'vinyl record' is a pressed black disc of seven, ten or 12 inches in diameter, containing music cut into the surface. Before CDs, and later MP3 files, vinyl records were the most popular format for selling pre-recorded music. Many DJs and music fans still buy and use vinyl records.

**Waveform**
A visual representation of sound, so-called because it rises and falls, in peaks and troughs, like a wave. If you load a song into music editing or DJ software, it will be displayed as a waveform.

# INDEX

# PICTURE CREDITS

**Ableton:** 82;
**Akai:** 79b, 138b;
**Alamy:** 35 (Miroslav Dakov), 39l (Chuan D. Vo/Zuma), 55 (Image Broker), 70/71 (Zuma), 75 (PYMCA), 80/81 (Debbie Bragg), 83t (Fotograferen), 85 (WENN), 88 (Cisco Pelay), 89b (EPA), 91 (WENN), 92 (EPA), 93 (Fotograferen), 94/95 (DPA Picture Alliance), 98 (Mirrorpix), 99 (PYMCA), 100 (Rob Ball), 106/107 (Fotograferen), 109t (David Woolfall), 109b (Ian Cartwright Lifestyle), 110 (Radius Images), 111t (Stephen Barnes/Law & Order), 114t (Arcaid Images), 119 (Melbourne Etc), 120 (Radharc Images), 123 (Robert Fisher), 127t (Marlene Ford), 127c (David Giral), 127b (EPA), 133b (Fotograferen), 134/135 (Zuma), 136t (Mike Abrahams), 138t (Lebrecht);
**Alamy/Everynight Images:** 60l, 89t, 96, 97, 101, 121t; **Avid:** 141t;
**Demensia:** 32bl;
**Depositphotos:** 14/15 (Pashapixel), 17c (Kavring), 22/23 (Kiriak 09), 33bl (Colour), 36/37 (Daxaio Productions), 102 (Piccia), 103t (Sirylok), 103b (Pozezan), 112l (New Light), 113b (Sylda Productions), 116 (FLP Photo), 117 (Artfotos), 121b (Salajean), 129tr (Michael Db), 129b (Vittore), 130 (Gpointstudio), 131t (Monkey Business), 131b (Wave Break Media), 133t (Corepics), 137b (Corepics), 140 (Zzoplanet);
**Fotolia:** 8/9 (Pavel Losevsky), 38 (Oneinchpunch);

**Getty Images:** 6t (Daniel Boczarski), 7tl (PYMCA), 7tr (Rob Loud), 21 (Barry Brecheisen), 39r (Jim Dyson), 56/57 (PYMCA), 60r (Michael Tullberg), 61 (PYMCA), 69 (Steve Grayson), 72 (Hayley Madden), 73 (Joseph Okpako), 83b (C Flanigan), 86/87 (David Wolff-Patrick), 105 (Redferns), 108 (PYMCA), 111b (Reggie Casagrande), 124/125 (Future Music/Adam Gasson), 126 (Scott Dudelson), 128 (Johnny Nunez/Wireimage), 129tl (Kevin Mazur/Wireimage), 132 (Rob Monk/Future Music), 139t (C. Brandon/Redferns), 139b (Theo Wargo/Wireimage for Bragman Wyman Cafarelli);
**Korg:** 79t;
**Novation:** 79c;
**Numark:** 16l, 76/77;

**Photoshot:** 90 (Retna), 137t (Andy Cantillon/Retna);
**Pioneer:** 7b, 16r, 17t, 27, 78, 84;
**Stanton:** 15b;
**Steinberg:** 141b;
**Tascam:** 112r;
**Technics:** 6b;
**Traktor:** 76;
**Zoom:** 33br

All other photographs were taken by Mark Wilkinson and are © Amber Books Ltd

We would like to thank Tom at BES Systems Ltd Bristol for Supplying the CDJ 2000 Nexus and Oli at Scratch Pro Audio (AKA DJ Five-stylez) for supplying equipment and modeling.